MANUEL NERI

A Sculptor's Drawings

MANUEL NERI

A Sculptor's Drawings

Space and Color in Paper: A Sculptor's Drawings
Jack Cowart

Manuel Neri's Early Sketchbooks
Price Amerson

The Corcoran Gallery of Art
Washington, D.C.

© 1994 The Corcoran Gallery of Art

ISBN 0-88675-041-5

Catalogue concept, research, and project coordination by
    Anne Kohs & Associates, Inc., San Francisco
Produced by Marquand Books, Inc., Seattle
Designed by Ed Marquand
Edited by Lorna Price, with assistance from
    Jessica Altholz Eber
Printed in Hong Kong

Photography by M. Lee Fatherree, Oakland,
except where noted.

Cover: *Pisano No. 9,* 1982.
Page vii: Untitled (Female Figure), 1958.

CONTENTS

FOREWORD

JACK COWART

Manuel Neri: A Sculptor's Drawings is a select exhibition chosen to celebrate almost four decades of evocative draftsmanship by a broadly talented sculptor. These works are more than notional studies for a wide range of sculptural projects. Many achieve a status of cherished independent works of art. They are large, beautiful, and exciting drawings. Encompassing almost every artistic "trick of the trade," they also show Neri intelligently, urgently, and creatively probing all areas of color, form, materials, and the nature of graphic invention.

We are especially grateful to Manuel Neri for his support of this project. He has opened his deep archive of historic and contemporary sketchbooks and other drawings, allowing us full access for both the catalogue and show. His patient sharing of biographical details and artistic anecdote has helped in many ways to set the record straight. Price Amerson deserves special mention for his devotion and insight concerning Neri's early sketchbooks and their preservation. He has displayed great perception in putting together again the many parts of the artist's past while not losing Neri's flair for the present and future. Thanks also to the many researchers in the firm of Anne Kohs and Associates, San Francisco, and especially to the principal, Anne Kohs, for critical assistance with the myriad logistical and catalogue details. The Exhibition Services Department and the Registrars of the Corcoran Gallery of Art have continued this project as an important part of our museum's national exhibition agenda.

I feel privileged to have been let loose in Neri's domain, where within one six-month period I could freely select not only this drawings survey but a companion exhibition of critical early sculpture. Much remains to be learned about the relations of so-called Bay Area art to national and international artists and art history, but I hope this historic exhibition sampling will raise the level of scholarly and aesthetic discourse. There is clearly much more here than meets the eye.

Opposite:
Alberica No. 19, 1990.

ix

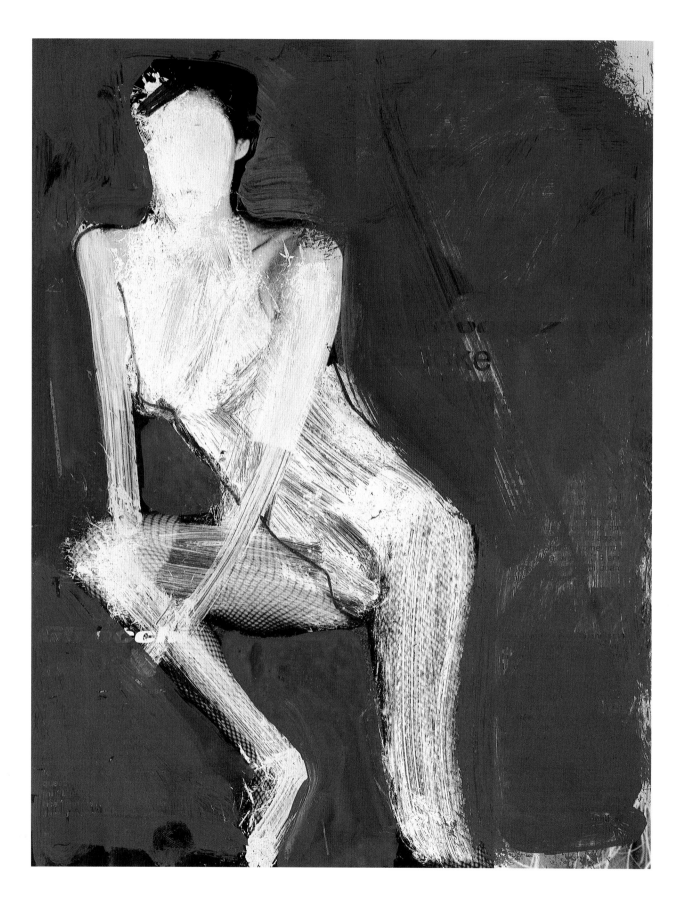

SPACE AND COLOR IN PAPER: A SCULPTOR'S DRAWINGS

JACK COWART

The drawings of Manuel Neri are wonderfully lush, almost romantic, excursions into the many worlds of the artist. These independent sheets and sketchbooks range broadly from elegant line drawings to palpably thick, expressive, layered and painterly renderings. They are the record of an artist anxiously, constantly, experimenting and visualizing his craft.

Neri's sculpture is his obliged public side. Every time he begins to build an armature and lay on plaster, it implies an explicit artistic performance and physical presence. Yet he also acts to deny this by carving, hacking, and gouging the plaster away. This is a reductive act, seemingly directed at minimizing any figurative connotations. He subtracts material in search of his own elusive creative essence or that occasioned by the model. In the process, the sculpture may be reduced to a ruin of powder. It may disappear, the discontented artist never having found the desired, magical balance. We can no longer reference what was taken away, or how, in works over-carved or worked to oblivion.

Neri's drawings are his private side, but they leave a more tangible, persuasive trail of positive action. His hundreds and hundreds of large and small sheets comprise a rich tapestry of recorded artistic thought. These works are additive, where strokes or colors are laid over others, built up in numerous mixed media. Collage elements of cut-and-pasted papers are frequently added. He rarely erases, but instead overdraws, giving the viewer a sense of the many cumulative and energetic decisions made along the way.

Drawings are materially cheap, easy to make and transport. Virtually all artists sketch, during pauses in their other work, when traveling, dining, talking, anytime. The eye and mind and hand are linked in drawing, as outlets for energy, disciplined or random thought, and as this artist's particular limbering up and planning exercises prior to his sculptural (public) performances. But more than mere construction blueprints, or a pianist's practiced scales, the artist's act of drawing results in something else: a formal artwork with its own enduring character of aesthetic beauty.

Neri's drawings depict fascinating aspects of the artist's ideas, feelings, and active exploration of mass, outline, color, and visual effects. They map out themes and variations, models posed this way and that (literally in the studio), or imagined through his mind's eye, or in a number of late 1970s drawings, reworked upon found fashion magazine photographs. His forms

Opposite:
1. *Gesture Study No. 81,* 1980.

1

shift endlessly, quickly and economically. Sometimes the backgrounds are white, then switched to black, playing positive against negative spaces. He includes theatrical lighting effects and forced points of view, often from below or tightly cropped. Dilute washes of ink or watercolor make flowing clouds or pools of radiant color, overdrawn with figures or forms. Each of these many drawings retains the mark of the artist's intuitively sculptural hand.

As the private works of a public sculptor, many of the drawings are nonetheless consciously artistic and seem intended for display as, perhaps, the artist's most "painterly" products. Having been advised in the late 1950s by his Bay Area artist-painter friends, in effect, to stop painting and focus more on sculpture, Neri may, by now, have achieved some sweet revenge with his drawings. They are arguably his most successful painted works. Perhaps his colleagues meant that Neri should stop putting oil paint on canvas and, instead, put it elsewhere. Indeed, from his earliest days, the artist has exhibited a distinct talent for the exploitation of color, whether applied to sculpture or paper. And now the painterly expression of his ink wash, watercolor, and gouache brushstrokes, and the loaded veils of stunning chromatic juxtapositions confirm de facto painting of the first order.

Of course, these are drawings still composed by a sculptor who is inclined to hatch and visually carve out deeply colored space on the page. Neri frequently applies broad background strokes in the general shape of the model or abstract form, then directly overdraws it, giving it a contour. He thus works cumulatively, out toward the viewer's world, adding element on element, searching for that telling contour, mentally rotating his image in a notional space. Unlike a traditional painter, Neri seems less worried about shallow planar composition or what happens at the edges.

The Later Drawings

Prevalent in the drawings made after 1976, Neri deposits the figure convincingly in the middle of the sheet. These works evolve a consistent, purposeful, and repetitive format. It is as if the artist intentionally created a template, something remote or iconic as the standard point of departure and formal challenge. These sheets are generally forty inches high by thirty inches wide and begin with a standing figure, a shape usually not lost even under the artist's repeated re-drawing and applied lush backgrounds of color, brush, and crayon markings. Whereas earlier drawings ranged widely in type, posture, and composition, Neri now seems hypnotically focused on one image, a tight totemic form hovering centrally in a rectangle filled otherwise with expressive painterly effects.

These current forms, rather Cycladic and Archaic in attitude, may evolve from two more contemporary sources. First, since the mid-1970s, Neri has been devoting each summer to making marble sculptures in Carrara, Italy. Carving monolithic blocks of hard stone leaves far fewer opportunities for expressive or extreme gesture when compared to his earlier plasters built on extended steel armatures. The marble forms are inherently more compact, arms tightly at the side, legs together, posed upright. The artist still continues his lifelong fight against the control of any material, "distressing" the surfaces with chisel blows, making areas of texture, and overpainting with high color, but this still has a physical limit. In his drawings of this period Neri can be seen to "distress" the backgrounds, swirling in paint and gestural markings, enjoying, it seems, his release from the restrictions of marble to reach a much more painterly and dramatic exercise in complex graphic and pictorial thinking.

Second, the extreme central figure may be further evidence of the indelible image left on his art by the model Mary Julia. So many works during, and after, the *Remaking of Mary Julia* sculptures of 1976 seem dictated by her particular physiognomy and the psychological challenges of their mutually competitive artist/model dialogues. These attitudes set the stage for Neri's late-1970s work, and her body-type surely provides the intuitive or subversive module even when the artist has worked from another subject.

Neri's recent monumental drawings are created in numbered suites named after places or things. While not strictly serial, each of these groups implies a given theme or setting, followed by several variations within that established dialect of elements. From 1980 to 1993, among the most important are: 1980—*Corazon, Indios Verdes, Carriona, Torano;* 1982—*K.C.;* 1987—*Isla Negra;* 1988—*Vicola, La Palestra;* 1989/1990—*Alberica, She Said;* 1991—*Agatas de Isla Negra, Claire;* 1992—*Agosin, Morena, Prietas, Dos Figuras-B/L;* 1993—*Recuerdo, Recuerdo Benicia.*

The early 1980s *K.C.* suite alternates red and black standing figures, some with green highlights, set against either unpainted or exuberantly brushed backgrounds. *K.C. No. 1, 1982,* is the most visually complex, the stalk-like bright red central model being thickly dripped, splashed, or brushed on first, followed by thinned black pigment broadly scumbled about it, all the way to the margins of the sheet. Neri exploits the effects where, by his designed chance, pools of black paint and water emulsion dry, leaving granular, soft puddles quite in contrast to surrounding heavier brushstrokes. The rectangle of the sheet cramps the tall figure, the artist having composed with little space above the head or below the feet. This effect of compression seems to bend the model, with the knees flexed. Irregular white shapes, areas left unpainted, serve as lively highlights, giving the form mass and energy contrary to its otherwise planar and static disposition.

Untitled Drawing No. 6, 1984, is another of Neri's classicized figures, now with the model's head hitting the top of the sheet. This large standing kouros type, with a slightly hipshot pose, is heavily overworked by pastel and crayon. The artist now uses dry, oily, and chalky media, seeking an opposite effect from that of the *K.C.* series. Layer after layer of pigment is built up, creating a dense web of lines, outlines, smudged and

4. *Vicola No. 4, 1987.*

3

5. *Alberica No. 1, 1989.*

Opposite left:
6. *Dos Figuras-B/L Series No. 2,*
   1992.

Opposite right:
7. *Recuerdo Benicia No. 8, 1993.*

Opposite bottom:
8. *Recuerdo Benicia No. 4, 1993.*

blended zones, and delicate tracery. It is these remarkable graphic inci-
dences in the draftsmanship, not necessarily its figural invention, which
provide the compelling visual attraction of this work.

The many *Alberica* series drawings explore opaque oil stick colors laid
on to create bright saturated backgrounds. *Alberica No. 1, 1989,* contra-

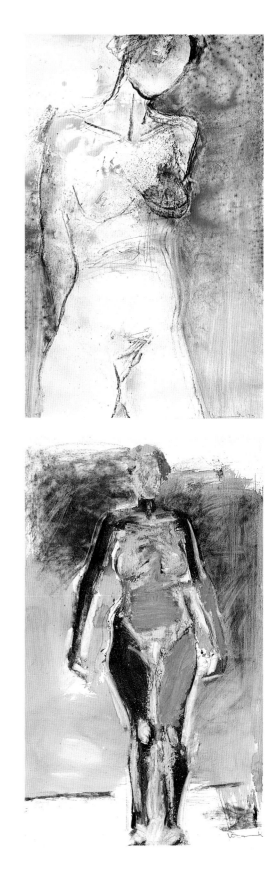

dicts others in this series by having been fully modeled in reds and blues, strongly projecting the figure out visually from the yellow sheet behind. Neri has radically sculpted and built a large crouched nude crammed into the drawing sheet rectangle. It is as oddly colored as any known work by the artist, or French *fauve*, for that matter.

The *Dos Figuras* series offers another rare break with the single-figure format so common in the 1980s and 1990s. Most drawings in the suite display two standing models rendered in mauve and black with ochre highlights. In *Dos Figuras-B/L Series No. 2, 1992,* Neri poses his models seated, tight into the lower right-hand corner. Charcoal and graphite are drawn over the dry pigment washes, reminding us that even as Neri lays in a background tone or area, he always seems to know the form that will be built later on the top layer. This is a remarkable and consistent quality, obviously the result of decades of work and observation.

Conclusion

Making artful drawings on paper may seem a bit too academically classical vis-à-vis our own contemporary technology or conceptual and vanguard environments. But Neri has most successfully pursued an art of exuberant handmade and revelatory character, content-laden in ways that are both contemporary and classical. His drawing is not necessarily about illustration or design but, rather, about quality of draftsmanship and mindful, if elusive, process. These works describe practice, discovery, refinement, energy, imagination, and evocative fantasy, and hermetic, obsessive, and preponderant activity. They are self-centered, very selfish in the best definition of the word, and very private stories when compared to his aggressively more public and exclamatory sculpture.

MANUEL NERI'S EARLY SKETCHBOOKS

PRICE AMERSON

Manuel Neri's sketchbooks provide a unique overview of the artist's interests and activities over almost forty years.[1] They also frequently provide insight into the artist and the development of his career as he works out and often reworks ideas and subjects. The sketchbooks thus become an invaluable resource for the historian as well as the biographer; they also become a fascinating record of the artist for the scholar, artist, or student. The sketchbooks reflect Neri's creative processes and the spontaneity and the dichotomies of his mind and hand, theory and practice, the rational and the intuitive.

From the surviving sketchbooks, it is clear that this activity begins early in his career; today, the artist continues this practice with a passion. For Neri, the sketchbooks collectively are a rich, sometimes dense overlay and repository of ideas and concerns. In the sketchbooks he explores initial ideas in quick sketches, which are at times accompanied by notes. Many of them evolve through successive stages and develop into more finished drawings and concepts. Others record more fleeting visual and written notes.

Many of Neri's fellow artists and former students relate how impressed they were that Neri was always sketching, whether he was the student or the teacher. Several sketchbooks seem to document class exercises done when he was a student, and others record studies he did as the teacher during a class assignment. Still others contain sketches related to the artist's domestic life and family activities. One may find names, addresses, and other similar notes juxtaposed with information on art materials, technical information, Neri's comments on his own works, or brief passages of poetry or philosophy; the blank sketchbook pages have also, from time to time, served the artist as a diary.

In addition to their freshness and immediacy, which often emerge in the entries whether visual or written, the sketchbooks also demonstrate the artist's spontaneity. One can follow Neri relentlessly pursuing an idea, and then laying the sketchbook down for a few minutes, or even abandoning it for a number of years, eventually returning to continue or rework sections in the same or different media. A series of studies may suddenly end or be interrupted; when the artist picks up the sketchbook again, he is interested in another subject or problem and thus fills the pages with studies that sometimes appear upside down with respect to previous sections. Or, he may decide to remove sheets, or even at times add collage, or cut

Opposite:
1. *Figure Study No. 54*, 1950s;
Reworked 1970s.

and tear sections of pages to edit the image or create "sculptural" overlays of images on successive pages. At first glance, a number of the sketchbooks may seem to be randomly filled, but they prove on closer examination to record various ideas that more or less date contemporaneously; it is not uncommon, however, to find sketchbooks that contain materials entered over a considerable period of time.

The earliest extant sketchbook is an appropriated printed reference book entitled (in retrospect, perhaps ironically) *Catalogue of Reprints in Series Sketchbook.*[2] Utilizing a variety of media—graphite, acrylic, charcoal, and gouache—Neri filled the printed pages with study after study for sculpture. Primarily the forms explore abstracted linear, open constructions to be made of eucalyptus wood. Color is a consistent concern; frequently forms are spontaneously fashioned by large areas of orange wash and controlled by the line of colored pencil in bold contrast to the regular columns of printed type on the pages. Occasionally Neri's studies will be executed in black wash, thus becoming more calligraphic and somewhat similar to Franz Kline's well-known studies on Manhattan telephone book pages.[3]

2. *Catalogue of Reprints in Series Sketchbook,* pages 108–109, c. 1953.

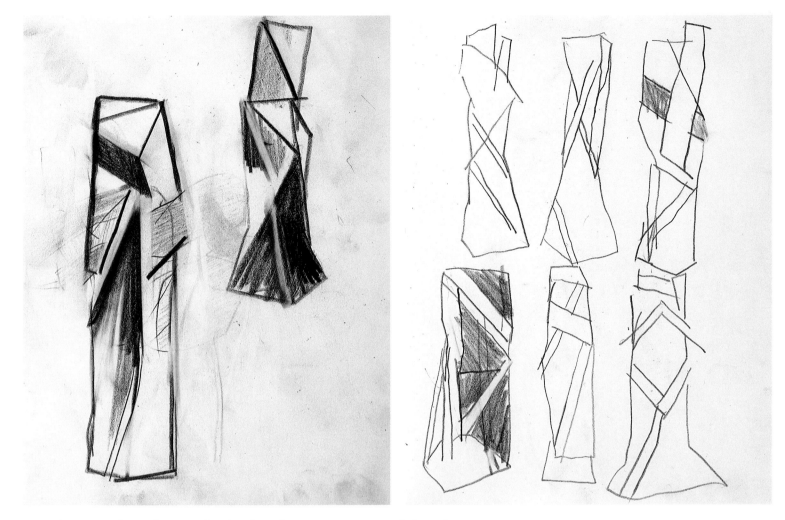

The artist dates these early sketches from circa 1953, and thus they were executed before he served a two-year hitch in Korea in the U.S. Army.[4] These sketches anticipate points of departure in his work after his return in 1955, when he made a firm commitment to art. Specifically, the works demonstrate Neri's assimilation and experience in working with Peter Voulkos and the discovery of expressive and gestural energy invested anew in the traditional forms and functions of ceramics. The sketches, along with numerous other sketchbooks from later in the decade, not only serve to document Neri's early ideas, but also record early sculptures that were realized but no longer survive. In several sketchbooks *(Raoul Sketchbook, Clipper Sketchbook, Casting Sketchbook),* numerous ideas are recorded for a series of cardboard and plaster sculptural abstract monoliths that the artist called "stelae." While we know that a number of these works were executed after 1958 and were even exhibited at the San Francisco Museum of Art in 1959 and the Dilexi Gallery in 1960,[5] it is primarily the sketchbooks, along with other loose drawings that were at one time undoubtedly parts of sketchbooks, which preserve this period of sculptural activity.[6]

Left:
3. *Raoul Sketchbook,* page 12, c. 1955–59.

Right:
4. *Raoul Sketchbook,* page 30 (verso), c. 1955–59.

Opposite:
5. *Clipper Sketchbook*,
   page 23, c. 1959.

Top left:
6. *Clipper Sketchbook*,
   page 21, c. 1959.

Top right:
7. *Clipper Sketchbook*,
   page 22, c. 1959.

Bottom:
8. *Clipper Sketchbook*,
   page 25, c. 1959.

Left:
9. *Casting Sketchbook,*
   page 55, c. 1959.

Right:
10. *Raoul Sketchbook,*
    page 27 (verso), c. 1955–59.

Opposite:
11. *Casting Sketchbook,*
    page 51, c. 1959.

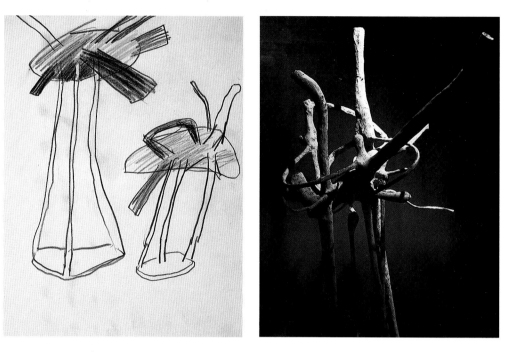

Thus in the sketchbooks one is able to trace Neri's development in and from the earlier abstract eucalyptus-branch sculptures through another group of studies of organic and anthropomorphic forms and energy with which the artist makes the notation "green trees" *(Green Trees Sketchbook)*. The latter sketches are undoubtedly connected to a body of works described as "plant-like constructions," which were shown at The 6 Gallery in 1957.[7] They and the previously noted organic and abstracted structural forms anticipate and provide transition into the colorful, abstracted-loop ceramic and plaster sculptures of the early 1960s for which Neri subsequently received considerable attention, since some of these pieces were included in exhibitions that received national notice.[8] The ceramic and plaster sculptures seem to have evolved from and no doubt concurrently with an impressive series of collage and color-wash studies that appear repeatedly in the *SFAI Sketchbook* and occasionally in the *Clipper Sketchbook*. On many of these sheets, Neri uses color and torn pieces of paper to experiment with and "sculpt" form and structure. Neri has stated that the possibilities of "color and three-dimensional form" he found in the ceramic medium were "very important to his development and it [ceramics] still is."[9]

Such drawings also reflect the artistic milieu of the San Francisco Bay Area within which the young artist had begun to interact, and in which he subsequently emerged as a major contributor. It thus is not surprising to find an occasional sketch related to the wood constructions of contemporary sculptors Alvin Light *(Raoul Sketchbook)* and Arlo Acton *(Green Trees Sketchbook)*.[10]

Left:
12. *Green Trees Sketchbook*, page 4, c. 1955–58.

Center:
13. *Green Trees Sketchbook*, page 12, c. 1955–58.

Right:
14. Untitled, 1955–56.

Opposite:
15. *Green Trees Sketchbook*, page 16, c. 1955–58.

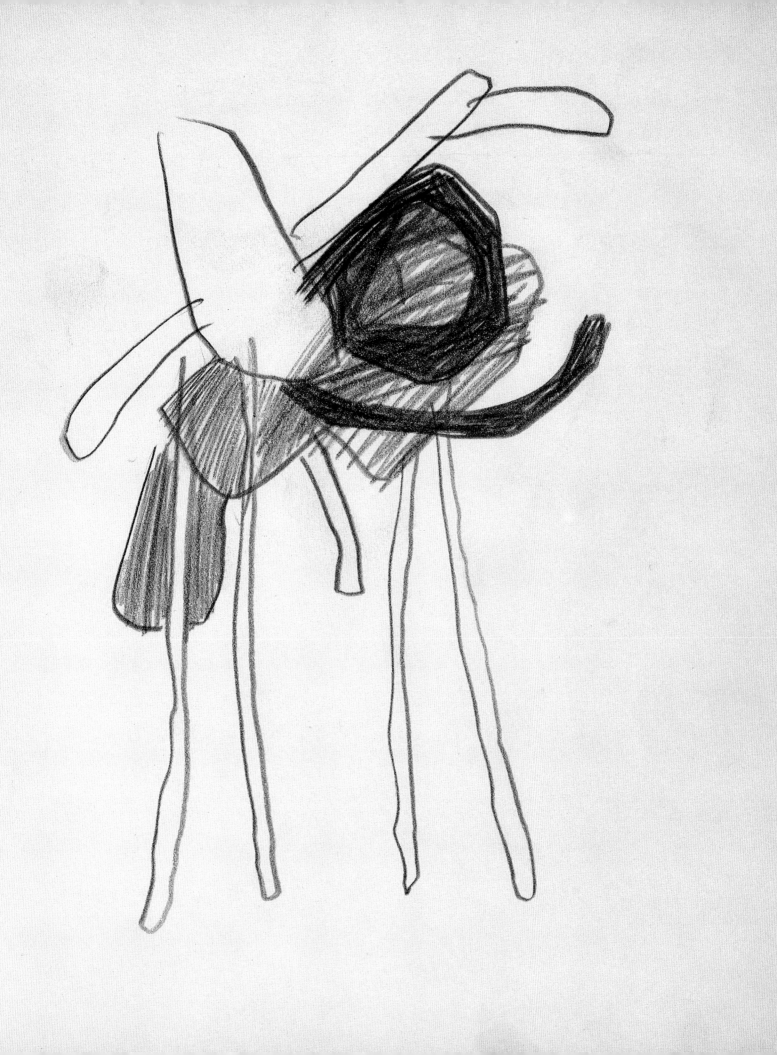

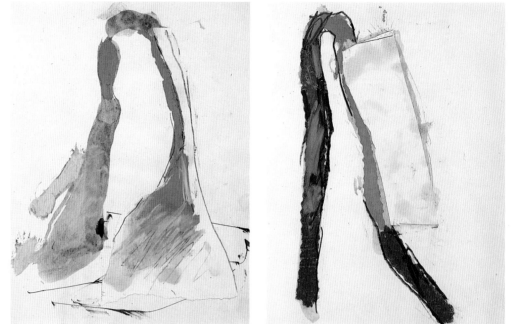

The sketchbooks also reveal early interests in contemporary European art. Juxtaposed with a variety of subjects in the *Landscapes Sketchbook* are two quick studies derived from reproductions of sculptures by Alberto Giacometti which, at the time, Neri would have seen as recent works by the Swiss sculptor. Neri's interest in European artists is usually discussed after he and Joan Brown traveled together in Europe in 1961. The work of Giacometti is frequently cited as an influence on Neri's later figurative sculpture. These sketches are fascinating in that the figure in Giacometti's sculpture is not emphasized by the young Neri; rather, it is form and relationships of shapes, space, and scale that are quickly analyzed.

If later sketchbooks from the decade of the 1950s and early 1960s reaffirm Neri's early explorations of abstracted conceptual forms and ideas, they also demonstrate his increasing interest in the human figure and especially its potential as a formal and expressive subject. In general, Neri's ventures into abstract compositions relate to the waning hold that abstract expressionism had on Bay Area painters and sculptors; the figurative works relate to the emerging interest among numerous artists and the development in the late 1950s of what is generally referred to as Bay Area figurative art. Many of the artists still associated with this transitional period in Bay Area art were Neri's teachers and/or contemporaries.[11] For Neri, the divergent styles and subjects were interrelated rather than separated and served to fuse and mold distinctive characteristics of his art.

Figurative sketchbooks from the late 1950s—*Casting Sketchbook, Fair Play Compositions Sketchbook* and *Etter Sketchbook*—record a variety of sessions with the live model, whether in the figure-drawing classroom or

Left:
16. *SFAI Sketchbook*, page 16, 1958–60.

Center:
17. *SFAI Sketchbook*, page 8, 1958–60.

Right:
18. *SFAI Sketchbook*, page 57, 1958–60.

Opposite:
19. *SFAI Sketchbook*, page 60, 1958–60.

Top left:
20. *Casting Sketchbook,*
    page 8, c. 1959.

Top center:
21. *Casting Sketchbook,*
    page 7, c. 1959.

Top right:
22. *Casting Sketchbook,*
    page 9, c. 1959.

Bottom left:
23. *Casting Sketchbook,*
    page 21, c. 1959.

Bottom center:
24. *Casting Sketchbook,*
    page 31, c. 1959.

Bottom right:
25. *Casting Sketchbook,*
    page 60, c. 1959.

from group figure-drawing sessions with other artists—Joan Brown, William H. Brown, Gordon Cook, and Alvin Light.[12] The figure may be studied repeatedly for form and pose, but just as consistently, there is a growing concern with the attitude and psychology of limbs, posture, and movement, which anticipates concerns that become central to Neri's figurative works of the late 1970s. In a few instances, one has a sequence of sketchbook sheets *(Figure Studies Sketchbook)* that show the model rendered in wash in the 1950s and then, almost twenty years later, the same figures are reworked and transformed with oil stick. *Green Trees Sketchbook* also contains some studies which seem more directly related to Neri's early efforts in figurative sculpture; two pages show several mask-like faces in profile which seem to be related to heads and busts executed by the artist during this decade in various materials—wire, cloth, wood, and plaster—and thus anticipate the expressive figural vocabulary developed subsequently in Neri's work.[13]

26. *Fair Play Compositions Sketchbook,* page 25, c. 1959.

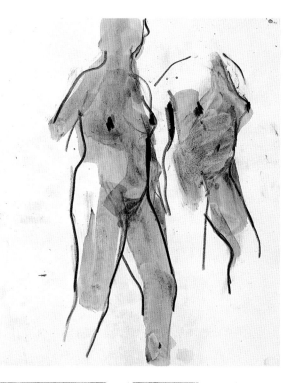

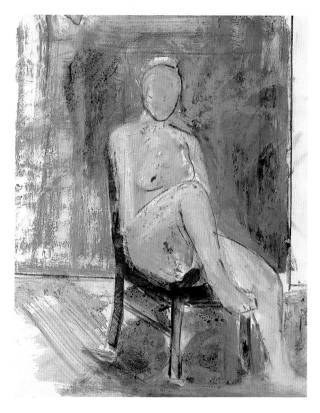

Opposite:
27. *Etter Sketchbook*, page 68,
   c. 1959.

Top left:
28. *Figure Study No. 34*, 1950s;
   Reworked 1970s.

Top right:
29. *Figure Study No. 53*, 1950s;
   Reworked 1970s.

Bottom left:
30. *Figure Study No. 4*, 1950s;
   Reworked 1970s.

Bottom right:
31. *Figure Study No. 33*, 1950s;
   Reworked 1970s.

In the later *Repair Sketchbook,* a series of pages is dominated by studies of heads in profile. In general, these seem to relate to numerous plaster heads, many of them titled after literary figures, executed by the artist in the decade of the 1970s. Several of the sketches, as well as some found in *Unos Actos de Fe Sketchbook,* however, can be closely associated with even later works, specifically a series of painted bronze heads from 1981–83 based on the model Makiko Nakamura.

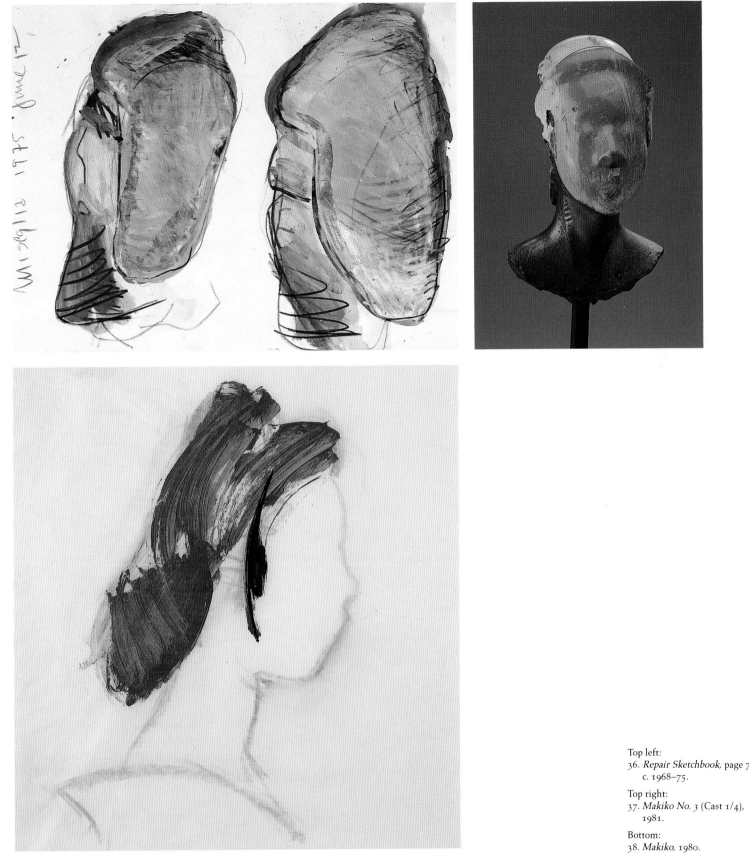

Top left:
36. *Repair Sketchbook,* page 72,
    c. 1968–75.

Top right:
37. *Makiko No. 3* (Cast 1/4),
    1981.

Bottom:
38. *Makiko,* 1980.

Other faces on sheets in this sketchbook are distinctive in the figure's pronounced nose. This feature seems to reflect a synthesis of a diverse number of "portraiture" sources, some of which had long fascinated the artist and range from ancient Tarentum clay grotesque masks, to Egyptian mummies with their "exposed" large noses, to features of life models that informed his work at this time.

Opposite:
39. *Repair Sketchbook,* page 77 (verso), c. 1968–75.

Top left:
40. *Repair Sketchbook,* page 83, c. 1968–75.

Top center:
41. *Repair Sketchbook,* page 74, c. 1968–75.

Top right:
42. *Repair Sketchbook,* page 81, c. 1968–75.

Bottom left:
43. *Repair Sketchbook,* page 78, c. 1968–75.

Bottom right:
44. *Repair Sketchbook,* page 79, c. 1968–75.

Top:
45. *Landscapes Sketchbook,*
      page 2, c. 1955–56.

Bottom:
46. *Casting Sketchbook,*
      page 1, c. 1959.

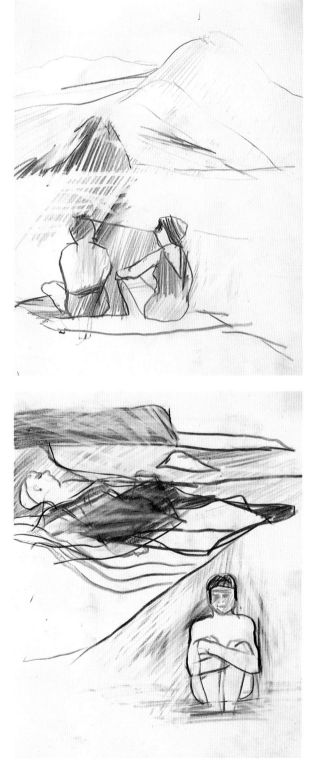

Several sketchbooks address a wide range of subjects, of which some are not commonly associated with the artist's works. As early as the mid-1950s one finds numerous pages devoted to quick graphite studies of observed landscapes *(Landscapes Sketchbook)*. Graphite studies of figures, animals, and seagulls, individually and in landscape settings, appear periodically in at least two sketchbooks of the late 1950s, *Casting Sketchbook* and *Fair Play Compositions Sketchbook,* and provide an alternative to sketches more commonly associated with the studio. The latter sketchbooks suggest their origin in events of the artist's private life—family outings or travel journals.

Top right:
48. *Fair Play Compositions Sketchbook,* page 3, c. 1959.

Top left:
47. *Fair Play Compositions Sketchbook,* page 16, c. 1959.

Bottom:
49. *Fair Play Compositions Sketchbook,* page 17, c. 1959.

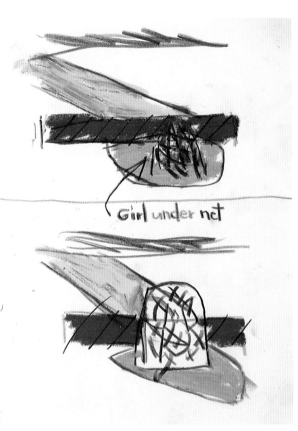

Girl under net

Top left:
50. *Fair Play Compositions Sketchbook,* page 29, c. 1959.

Top right:
51. *Fair Play Compositions Sketchbook,* page 28, c. 1959.

Bottom left:
52. *Fair Play Compositions Sketchbook,* page 26, c. 1959.

Bottom right:
53. *Fair Play Compositions Sketchbook,* page 27, c. 1959.

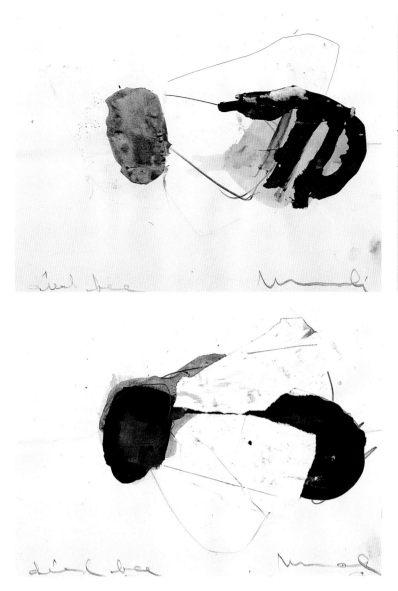

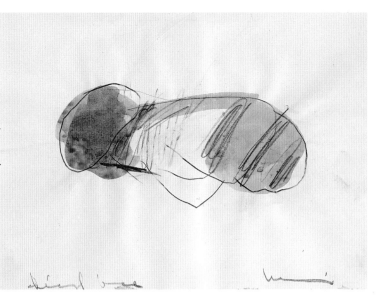

In *Fair Play Compositions Sketchbook,* one finds colorful sketches which, at first glance, suggest Neri's early painted plaster and cardboard sculptures. The studies however are for stage sets designed by the artist for San Francisco's American Conservatory Theater (A.C.T.) and its production of Jean Cocteau's drama *The Infernal Machine.* According to the artist, he immediately rushed out to get a copy of the play when asked to design the sets, and soon became totally absorbed in the surrealist tragedy and in creating sets appropriate for Cocteau's "strange, large monster magic."[14]

Other books preserve sketches that can easily be classified as still life and reveal interests rarely discussed in connection with Neri's work. In *Stick Sketchbook,* a series of pages of abstracted, organic forms sensitively studied and beautifully rendered in ink and wash is thoughtfully identified for us by the artist as a "dried bee."

Top left:
54. *Stick No. 46,* c. 1970.
Top right:
55. *Stick No. 43,* c. 1970.
Bottom:
56. *Stick No. 51,* c. 1970.

Another sketchbook, *Rock*, contains an equally impressive series of still-life studies. The subject, a coffee pot and other kitchen tools and utensils, is explored repeatedly in terms of line and form with varying emphases on both the positive and negative areas and relationships of the objects in the composition. The set-up may well have been composed by Neri for a drawing class in the Department of Art at the University of California, Davis, and the artist becomes absorbed in the problem as well. One of the sketches is accompanied by a note of criticism: "too small/not using the space of your paper/get a camera . . ."

In sketchbooks dating from the late 1950s *(Fair Play Compositions Sketchbook, Casting Sketchbook, Etter Sketchbook,* and *Figure Studies Sketchbook)*, one finds sketches that seem to reflect more domestic situations and to parallel Neri's early association with Joan Brown. Brown poses for concise figure studies; her dog is quickly rendered in several studies as it sleeps or "poses." Some of the sketches may even be by Joan Brown. A similar collaboration can be found in the *No Hands Neri Sketchbook.* A series of playful sketches involves the hand of Susan Morse, to whom Neri was married from 1967 to 1972; one of the sketches depicts a caricature of Neri with outstretched arms astride a bull, hence the inscription "No hands Neri."

Left:
57. *Rock No. 26,* c. 1967–74.

Right:
58. *Rock No. 27,* c. 1967–74.

No hands
Neri

Top left:
59. *Fair Play Compositions
Sketchbook,* page 79, c. 1959.

Top center:
60. *Casting Sketchbook,* page 22,
c. 1959.

Top right:
61. *Fair Play Compositions
Sketchbook,* page 73, c. 1959.

Bottom:
62. *No Hands Neri Sketchbook,*
page 6, c. 1964–66.

Top left:
63. *CSFA Sketchbook,* page 13,
    c. 1962–64.

Top right:
64. *CSFA Sketchbook,* page 5,
    c. 1962–64.

Bottom:
65. *Projections Sketchbook,*
    page 64, c. 1965–83.

Other sketchbooks contain a series of landscape studies which provide the artist's observations of the changing conditions of light and mood. A series of Clear Lake views (in Lake County, California) from the *CSFA Sketchbook* records spontaneous impressions of the interplay of atmospheric conditions and changes, and offers fascinating parallels with interests displayed in the same sketchbook in figure studies that focus on the spontaneity and change of the model's gestures. In this sketchbook are also sketches and collages that clearly relate to Neri's teaching activities at the San Francisco Art Institute (formerly the California School of Fine Arts) in 1963 and 1964.

Neri's engagement with landscape in the 1960s moves from depictions of the condition of a particular place, such as Clear Lake, to other sketchbooks (e.g., *Projections Sketchbook*) in which he records "Benicia Waterfront" and dates it "1965,"[15] to sites with archeological interest, sketches in which he records details from both memory and visual sources.

In the *No Hands Neri Sketchbook,* the artist will move from figure studies where the figure is isolated and/or paired to a series of studies for sculptures made of surplus steel and aluminum "blocks" that are also, in a parallel fashion, studied individually or paired. The latter studies, executed in both black and white and vivid color washes, relate to a period in Neri's work in which he investigated through countless drawings various sculptural ideas to be executed in more permanent materials while continuing to experiment with throw-away materials—cardboard, cloth, burlap, and plaster. Many of the works, both freestanding and wall-mounted pieces in impermanent materials, were realized and even exhibited, but today few remain in good condition.[16]

Left:
66. *No Hands Neri Sketchbook,*
    page 65, c. 1964–66.

Right:
67. *No Hands Neri Sketchbook,*
    page 66, c. 1964–66.

Top:
68. *Study No. 5 for Tikal Series I,* c. 1969.

Bottom:
69. *Repair Sketchbook,* page 33, c. 1968–75.

These sketchbooks date more or less contemporaneously with others in which the artist devotes page after page to a long-standing fascination with pre-Columbian sites, particularly Tikal and Tula, that he first visited in the 1950s with Billy Al Bengston. Visiting friends in Mexico City, Neri speaks of the interest this trip aroused in pre-Columbian architecture and other ancient cultures, an interest "especially in the setting of structure and architecture and a consciousness of the land and the relationship of land and vanished people who occupied the sacred areas and temples."[17]

The architectural forms and details of the stepped pyramid at Tula become the subject for several pieces executed for and related to "The Repair Show," an exhibition mounted in March and April of 1969 at the Berkeley Gallery, San Francisco, for which artists were asked to develop pieces on the theme of repair.[18] Neri included two large freestanding pieces entitled *The Great Steps of Tula* and *Monument for the Repair of a National Image*.[19] Using cardboard, plaster, lath, and chicken wire, the two pieces simultaneously evoke the stairstep facades of the Tula model, yet juxtapose the solidity of the forms with the fragility of the materials and the exposed open skeleton of their support framework. Even the juxtaposition of their titles seems to imply contrast and comparison of time, age, and cultural meaning.

70. Installation of "The Repair Show," March 13–April 14, 1969, Berkeley Gallery.

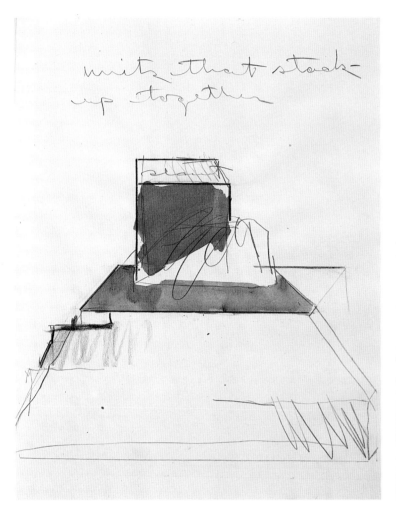

units that stack up together

At least one notebook *(Repair Sketchbook)* survives intact and contains numerous studies of Tula and Tikal; it documents the artist evolving ideas for pieces on the repair theme. Pencil and watercolor sketches of geometric architectural derivations from pre-Columbian monuments, and wash drawings of mysterious architectural fragments and settings populated, at times, by solitary figures, are juxtaposed with notes on sculpture. For example, the artist writes "repair of the great steps of Tula" on a drawing, then on subsequent pages notes "steps for repair show"; on other pages "slanting steps" and "steps into wall" appear with sketches, and then he notes with some resolution, "units that stack up together."

Left:
71. *Repair Sketchbook,* page 39,
    c. 1968–75.

Right:
72. *Repair Sketchbook,* page 40,
    c. 1968–75.

Opposite:
73. *Repair Sketchbook,* page 41,
    c. 1968–75.

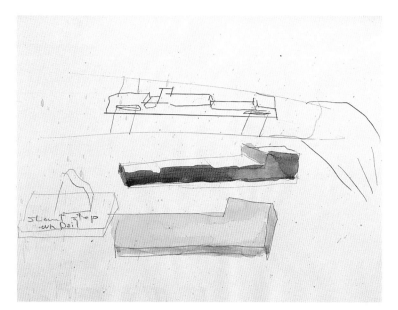

In the same sketchbook, Neri documents an interest in related sources. For example, the infamous "slant step" that intrigued and beguiled so many Bay Area artists in the late 1960s is not ignored by Neri.[20] Specific and more generalized references to this non-art object, a plywood and green linoleum "step" discovered and purchased in a salvage shop by William T. Wiley and Bruce Nauman in 1965, which subsequently inspired countless art objects, appear in several sketchbooks (see also *Stick Sketchbook* and *Projections Sketchbook*). Along with studies for the Tula steps and "The Repair Show," the "slant step's" sensuous profile is sketched, and one even finds written notations, e.g., "slant step sundial," which indicate Neri's consideration of pieces based on the "slant step."

Another thematic exhibition, "The Ladder Show," for which artists were asked to execute specific works, was mounted in October 1972 at the Artists Contemporary Gallery in Sacramento. Neri devotes a section of the *Ladder Sketchbook* to his concept for the show, a thin, elongated ladder in wood (20 ft. × 12 in.).[21] The subject and its formal and structural implications as well as his recent obsession with stepped sculptural forms inform Neri's ideas as he records them in graphite and watercolor. The studies, primarily emphasizing the regular but jagged profile of the piece, explore the ladder form as a single object and in parallel multiples. On one sketch page, Neri identifies the placement and installation of the piece in a corner; in another he writes "flying buttress" as an apparent structural analogy, but there is also a striking visual correspondence between the drawings of his ladder in profile and the familiar patterned device of Gothic cathedrals. In one of the drawings he carefully scribbles a word so that it "ascends" the steps of the ladder. Possibly "enlightenment" or "alignment," it perhaps was meant to provide metaphorical meaning to the utilitarian form.

Left:
74. *Repair Sketchbook,* page 71,
    c. 1968–75.

Right:
75. *Ladder Sketchbook,* page 17,
    1971–72.

Opposite:
76. *Ladder Sketchbook,* page 20,
    1971–72.

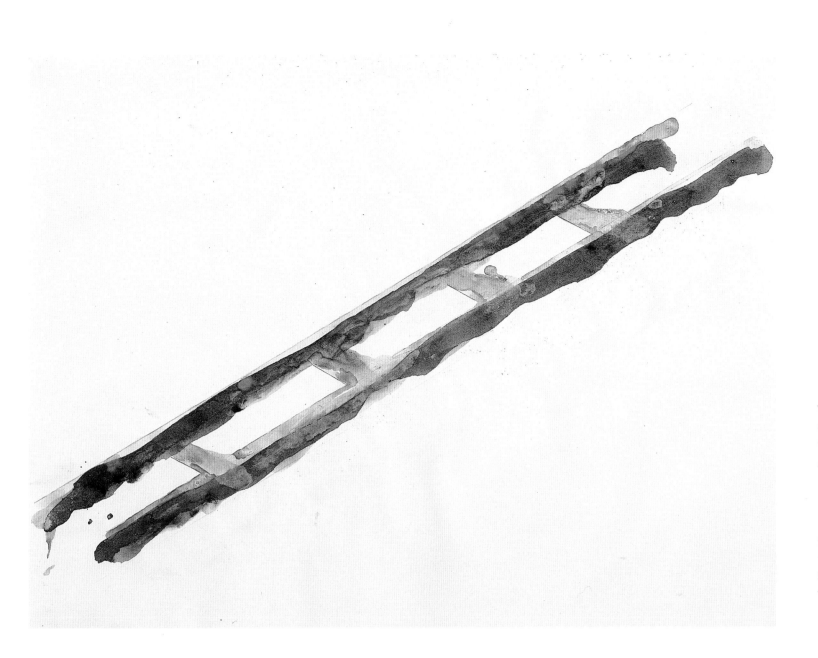

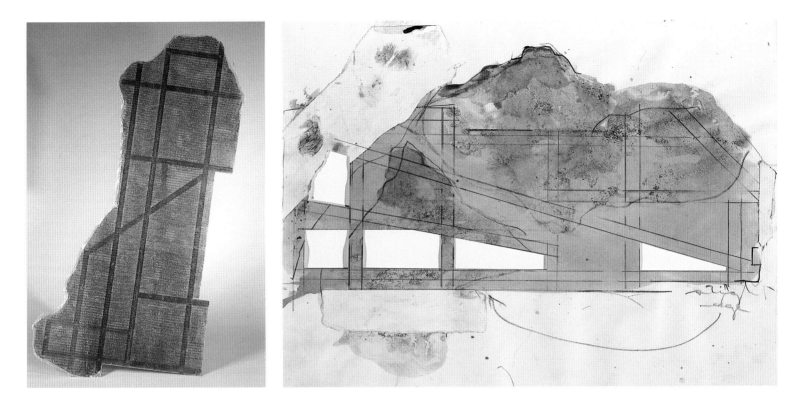

Variations on the basic form of vertical and slanted elements and the fascination with common materials pervade a significant part of Neri's sculpture and works on paper during the late 1960s and into the decade of the 1970s. The *Repair Sketchbook* contains numerous studies reflecting an ongoing interest in large wood and plaster constructions, which the artist identifies as "street grids" and "totems." References to "lead and glass" accompany many of the street-grid studies, which clearly suggest an architectural reference to lattice-type windows and, to Neri's mind, seem to have equivalents with "lath and fiberglass."

In the *Repair Sketchbook,* the artist makes significant notes that roughly correspond to his new interest in fiberglass as a sculptural medium. It is well known that Neri used fiberglass in a series of figure fragments cast from earlier plaster figures. These pieces were specifically part of a developing body of work for an exhibition at the San Francisco Museum of Art in the autumn of 1971.[22] He identifies and juxtaposes the words "fiberglass" and "stained glass" on successive pages, as if realizing and establishing an analogy between the two in terms of light and color and as formal aspects of the work to consider and reconsider.

Opposite:
77. *Repair Sketchbook,* page 57, c. 1968–75.

Left:
78. *Emborados Series—Nazca Lines V,* 1971.

Right:
79. *Repair Sketchbook,* page 59, c. 1968–75.

A sketchbook that apparently dates only a few years later and which contains a suite of figure studies for the Crucifixion intended for a Los Altos convent chapel *(Crucifixion Sketchbook)* contains Neri's notes for further pieces to be cast with plaster and rubber latex molds as well as other notes specifically to remind himself that "when reliefs are finished paint with resin and fiberglass."

This sketchbook and another, *Rock Sketchbook,* contain valuable studies and records of Neri's working methods for the Los Altos project. They also document early drawing sessions with model Mary Julia Raahauge. Through line and vivid wash, several of the drawings depict Mary Julia in various poses. These are juxtaposed with sheets on which Neri transposes the life drawings into depictions specifically related to the themes of the Crucifixion and Ascension.

Left:
80. *Crucifixion Sketchbook,*
    page 30 (verso), c. 1972–73.

Right:
81. *Rock No. 40,* c. 1967–74.

Opposite:
82. *Crucifixion Sketchbook,*
    page 24 (verso), c. 1972–73.

Opposite:
83. *Crucifixion Sketchbook,*
    page 22, c. 1972–73.

Top:
84. *Rock No. 6,* c. 1967–74.

Practical and philosophical notes continue frequently to accompany Neri's visual ideas. In the series of early studies for sculptures in the *Green Trees Sketchbook,* the artist notes structural solutions, for example, "thing is all held together by wire." In a later sketchbook *(No Hands Neri),* he strikes a more philosophical note: "I sometimes think it is not possible— but it does happen." In another book *(Ladder Sketchbook),* he notes "chopped up" followed by "forget it." On another sheet he again comments on a structural detail: "this stuck in cardboard wall"; on the back of the page he writes, "putting things down on paper/the life you want to control neatly placed side by side." Finally, in another sketchbook the artist repeatedly writes: "On bad days I stand here and everything is okay."

85. *Rock No. 44,* c. 1967–74.

NOTES

1. Over thirty sketchbooks have been located in the artist's collection; they form the basis of this study. Through the years other sketchbooks have been presumably lost or dismantled. I am indebted to Anne Kohs & Associates, and especially to Armelle Futterman, for unfailing assistance and many contributions to this study. For the sake of reference and identification, the sketchbooks have been titled recently according to (1) the first written entry and/or (2) the type of sketchbook used.

2. Seventh edition; edited by Robert M. Orton. New York: The H. W. Wilson Co., 1946. The book, deaccessioned by the California College of Arts and Crafts library, was purchased by Neri at an Oakland bookstore. Over fifty related sketches for eucalyptus sculptures are known that seem to date several years later, after Neri's return from Korea. Executed in colored inks and graphite and occasionally incorporating acrylic and crayon, the studies are on the reverse of mimeographed correspondence (11 × 8¼ in.) and on heavier paper (8¼ × 18 in.), the latter sheets removed from a ledger book at some point.

3. This is not intended to imply a direct source for Neri, but more of a correspondence in the relationship between the expressive stroke of the brush and the "found" printed-matter page. By this date, however, the young Neri was certainly aware of the work of some of the New York abstract expressionist artists, primarily through reproductions in magazines and exhibition catalogues. Calligraphy was of interest to Neri rather early on. He recalls that calligraphy by young Japanese artists, in particular, which he saw while serving in the U.S. Army from 1953–55, impressed him greatly. (Conversation with the artist, December 26, 1990.)

4. Conversation with the artist, December 26, 1990.

5. Neri's works were included in the exhibition "Four Man Show: Sam Francis, Wally Hedrick, Fred Martin, Manuel Neri," in February 1959 at the San Francisco Museum of Art; the Dilexi exhibition was in June–July 1960.

6. At least fifty single-sheet drawings survive, in graphite only as well as in graphite, ink, and pastel, representing studies for painted plaster and cardboard sculptures. The size (11 × 8 in.) and format of the sheets indicate that they were originally bound together as a sketchbook or sketchpad.

7. Two-person show with Jo-Ann Bentley Low in February–March 1957.

8. See John Coplans, *Abstract Expressionist Ceramics,* exhibition catalogue (Irvine: The Fine Arts Gallery, University of California, 1966), in which *Loop No. 1* and *Loop No. 2* are reproduced; these and *Loop No. 3* are cited in the exhibition checklist. See also Peter Selz, *Funk,* exhibition catalogue (Berkeley: University Art Museum, University of California, 1967), in which *Loop No. 1* is reproduced, and, with *Loop No. 2* and a plaster and cardboard *Moon,* is in the checklist. The date 1961 is cited for all works in both exhibitions. It is interesting to note that *Loop No. 1* and *Loop No. 2* were at that time in the collection of Peter Voulkos.

9. Conversation with the artist, December 26, 1990.

10. During this period Neri shared a studio with Alvin Light, as well as with Charles Ginnever.

11. Neri has commented several times on the more relaxed relationship between teacher and student in the late 1950s: "We were constantly learning from each other." (Conversation with the artist, December 26, 1990.)

12. From 1959–62 these artists met for weekly drawing sessions. Subsequently Neri participated in weekly drawing groups in 1969 and 1972–74 with Joan Brown, Gordon Cook, Robert Arneson, and Elmer Bischoff.

13. Probably the best known of the early busts is the painted plaster *Dr. Zonk,* dating from 1958. For discussion of this and later heads, see Caroline A. Jones, *Manuel Neri: Plasters,* exhibition catalogue (San Francisco: San Francisco Museum of Modern Art, 1989), p. 11ff.

14. Conversation with the artist, March 19, 1993.

15. The date corresponds with the year that Neri purchased and moved into an abandoned Congregational church in Benicia.

16. Aluminum and plaster boxes were exhibited at the Quay Gallery, San Francisco in 1968; "geometric sculptures" were shown at the San Francisco Art Institute in 1970.

17. Conversation with the artist, December 26, 1990. Elsewhere, Neri has stated, "I was intrigued by the way they [the pre-Columbian structures] imposed themselves on their environment as related to the conceptual ideas in contemporary art," cited in Caroline A. Jones, *Manuel Neri: Plasters,* pp. 19–20, n. 36.

18. Formed in 1964 in Berkeley as a cooperative gallery with monthly dues for artists, the Berkeley Gallery was mainly supported by Marian and Jim Wintersteen. The gallery moved to San Francisco in 1966 and gained notoriety for mounting "The Slant Step Show" in September. See *The Slant Step Revisited,* exhibition catalogue (Davis: Richard L. Nelson Gallery, University of California, 1983).

19. Works in the exhibition were photographed by Jack Fulton and spiral-bound as "catalogue" documentation for the show. The two cited works by Neri are the only two that appear in the photographic essay. There seems to be some confusion in the literature as to how many pieces by Neri were in the show. Jones, *Manuel Neri: Plasters,* p. 20, for example, notes: "Neri's contribution to the 'Repair Show' was a large environmental construction, evoking pre-Columbian architecture in the process of decay and resurrection." There is also a large-scale wall-piece construction of painted cardboard and wire mesh, *The Repair of the Great Steps of Tula,* which seems to date contemporaneously and at times was thought to have been included in the exhibition. We know that Neri also executed numerous small constructions of the steps cut from ink wash studies and mounted on mesh wire frameworks. Most of them, or at least the surviving pieces, seem to date a few years later and are testaments to his continuing fascination with the theme.

20. See the Nelson Gallery catalogue *The Slant Step Revisited* for this famous saga.

21. The show was organized by artist Darrell Forney, who also produced the catalogue, in which the entry for Neri's piece is noted as a late addition, and the piece is not illustrated.

22. See Gerald Nordland, *Arts of San Francisco: Manuel Neri,* exhibition brochure (San Francisco Museum of Art, 1971).

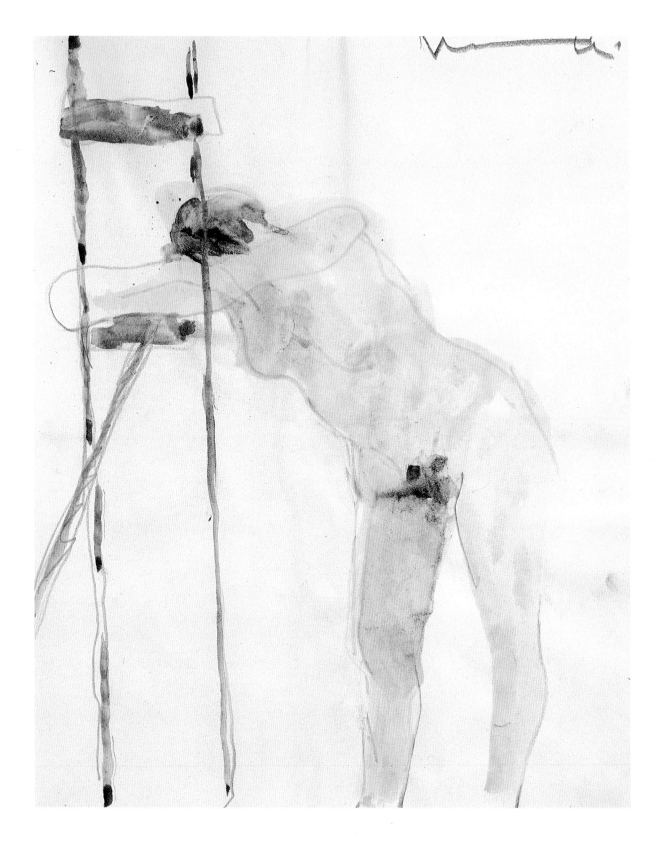

86. *Rock No. 45,* c. 1967–74.

LIST OF ILLUSTRATIONS

51. *Fair Play Compositions Sketchbook,* page 28, c. 1959
Graphite, oil pastel on paper
9⅞"h × 7⅝"w
52. *Fair Play Compositions Sketchbook,* page 26, c. 1959
Graphite, oil pastel on paper
9⅞"h × 7⅝"w
53. *Fair Play Compositions Sketchbook,* page 27, c. 1959
Graphite, oil pastel on paper
9⅞"h × 7⅝"w
54. *Stick No. 46,* c. 1970
Graphite, ink on paper
10⅞"h × 13⅞"w
55. *Stick No. 43,* c. 1970
Graphite, ink on paper
10⅞"h × 13⅞"w
56. *Stick No. 51,* c. 1970
Graphite, ink on paper
10⅞"h × 13⅞"w
57. *Rock No. 26,* c. 1967–74
Ink, graphite on paper
10½"h × 13⅝"w
58. *Rock No. 27,* c. 1967–74
Graphite, ink on paper
10½"h × 13⅝"w
59. *Fair Play Compositions Sketchbook,* page 79, c. 1959
Graphite on paper
9⅞"h × 7⅝"w
60. *Casting Sketchbook,* page 22, c. 1959
Graphite on paper
10⅞"h × 8½"w
61. *Fair Play Compositions Sketchbook,* page 73, c. 1959
Graphite on paper
7⅝"h × 9⅞"w
62. *No Hands Neri Sketchbook,* page 6, c. 1964–66
Graphite on paper
13⅞"h × 10¾"w
63. *CSFA Sketchbook,* page 13, c. 1962–64
Graphite, ink on paper
10⅝"h × 13½"w
64. *CSFA Sketchbook,* page 5, c. 1962–64
Graphite, ink on paper
10⅝"h × 13½"w
65. *Projections Sketchbook,* page 64, c. 1965–83
Graphite, ink on paper
10⅞"h × 13⅝"w
66. *No Hands Neri Sketchbook,* page 65, c. 1964–66
Graphite, ink, oil pastel on paper
13⅞"h × 10¾"w
67. *No Hands Neri Sketchbook,* page 66, c. 1964–66
Graphite, ink, oil pastel on paper
30"h × 22⅛"w
68. *Study No. 5 for Tikal Series I,* c. 1969
Graphite, ink, collage on paper
10½"h × 13⅝"w
69. *Repair Sketchbook,* page 33, c. 1968–75
Graphite, ink on paper
11"h × 14"w
70. Installation of "The Repair Show,"
March 13–April 14, 1969,
Berkeley Gallery. Photo by Jack Fulton
71. *Repair Sketchbook,* page 39, c. 1968–75
Graphite, ink on paper
14"h × 11"w
72. *Repair Sketchbook,* page 40, c. 1968–75
Graphite, ink on paper
14"h × 11"w
73. *Repair Sketchbook,* page 41, c. 1968–75
Graphite, ink on paper
14"h × 11"w
74. *Repair Sketchbook,* page 71, c. 1968–75
Graphite, ink on paper
11"h × 14"w
75. *Ladder Sketchbook,* page 17, 1971–72
Graphite, ink, collage on paper
10⅞"h × 13¾"w
76. *Ladder Sketchbook,* page 20, 1971–72
Graphite, ink on paper
10⅞"h × 13¾"w
77. *Repair Sketchbook,* page 57, c. 1968–75
Graphite, ink, collage on paper
14"h × 11"w
78. *Emborados Series—Nazca Lines V,* 1971
Wire mesh, wood, fiberglass, resin
97½"h × 51½"w × 1"d
79. *Repair Sketchbook,* page 59, c. 1968–75
Graphite, ink, collage on paper
14"h × 11"w
80. *Crucifixion Sketchbook,* page 30 (verso), c. 1972–73
Graphite, watercolor, ink on paper
13⅝"h × 10¾"w
81. *Rock No. 40,* c. 1967–74
Graphite, ink, watercolor on paper
13⅝"h × 10½"w
82. *Crucifixion Sketchbook,* page 24 (verso), c. 1972–73
Charcoal on paper
13⅝"h × 10¾"w
83. *Crucifixion Sketchbook,* page 22, c. 1972–73
Graphite, ink on paper
13⅝"h × 10¾"w
84. *Rock No. 6,* c. 1967–74
Graphite, ink on paper
13⅝"h × 10½"w
85. *Rock No. 44,* c. 1967–74
Graphite, ink on paper
13⅝"h × 10½"w
86. *Rock No. 45,* c. 1967–74
Graphite on paper
13⅝"h × 10½"w

BIOGRAPHY

BORN

1930   Sanger, CA

EDUCATION

1949–50   San Francisco City College
1951–52   University of California, Berkeley
1952–57   California College of Arts and Crafts, Oakland
1957–59   California School of Fine Arts, San Francisco

TEACHING

1959–65   California School of Fine Arts, San Francisco
1963–64   University of California, Berkeley
1965–90   University of California, Davis

GRANTS AND AWARDS

1953   Oakland Art Museum, First Award in Sculpture
1957   Oakland Art Museum, Purchase Award in Painting
1959   Nealie Sullivan Award, California School of Fine Arts, San Francisco
1963   San Francisco Art Institute, 82nd Annual Sculpture Award
1965   National Art Foundation Award
1970–75   University of California at Davis, Sculpture Grant
1979   Guggenheim Foundation Fellowship
1980   National Endowment for the Arts, Individual Artist Grant
1982   American Academy and Institute of Arts and Letters, Academy-Institute Award in Art
1985   San Francisco Arts Commission, Award of Honor for Outstanding Achievement in Sculpture
1990   San Francisco Art Institute, Honorary Doctorate for Outstanding Achievement in Sculpture
1992   California College of Arts and Crafts, Honorary Doctorate

COMMISSIONS

1980–82   Office of the State Architect, State of California, Commission for marble sculpture *Tres Marias* for The Bateson Building, Sacramento
1987   North Carolina National Bank, Commission for marble sculpture *Española* for NCNB Tower, Tampa, FL
        The Linpro Company, Commission for marble sculpture *Passage* for the Christina Gateway Project, Wilmington, DE
        U.S. General Services Administration, Commission for marble sculpture *Ventana al Pacífico* for U.S. Courthouse, Portland, OR
1994   Laumeier Sculpture Park, St. Louis, MO

SOLO EXHIBITIONS

1957   The 6 Gallery, San Francisco
1959   Spatsa Gallery, San Francisco
1960   Dilexi Gallery, San Francisco, June 20–July 16
1963   New Mission Gallery, San Francisco
1964   Berkeley Gallery, Berkeley, CA
1966   Quay Gallery, San Francisco, *Neri Sculpture*
1968   Quay Gallery, San Francisco
1969   Louisiana State University, Baton Rouge
1970   St. Mary's College, Moraga, CA
        San Francisco Art Institute
1971   Art Gallery, University of Nevada, Reno
        San Francisco Museum of Art, *Arts of San Francisco: Manuel Neri*, August 6–September 5. Brochure
        Quay Gallery, San Francisco, *Manuel Neri at Quay*, November 9–27
1972   Sacramento State College Art Gallery, Sacramento, CA, *Work by Manuel Neri*, March 22–April 18

Davis Art Center, Davis, CA, *Manuel Neri: New Sculpture*, October 27–November 16
1974   University Art Gallery, San Jose State University, San Jose, CA, February 13–March 8
        Davis Art Gallery, Stephens College, Columbia, MO, *Manuel Neri: Sculpture and Installations*, October 3–23
1975   Quay Gallery, San Francisco, *Manuel Neri: Sculpture and Drawings*, April 1–26
1976   Braunstein/Quay Gallery, New York, *Neri Sculpture*, March 16–April 10
        80 Langton Street, San Francisco, *The Remaking of Mary Julia: Sculpture in Process*, May 4–15
        The Oakland Museum, Oakland, CA, *Manuel Neri, Sculptor*, September 21–November 28. Travel to Utah Museum of Fine Arts, Salt Lake City, March 12–May 1, 1977. Catalogue
1977   ArtSpace/Open Ring, E. B. Crocker Art Gallery, Sacramento, CA, *Manuel Neri: Recent Sculpture and Drawings*, July 22–August 20. Catalogue
1979   Gallery Paule Anglim, San Francisco, *Manuel Neri*, May 15–June 9
1980   Whitman College, Walla Walla, WA, *Manuel Neri: Sculpture and Drawings*, April 1–30
        Richmond Art Center, Richmond, CA, *Manuel Neri: Drawings*, July 1–31
        Grossmont College Gallery, El Cajon, CA, *Manuel Neri*, November 10–December 10
1981   Seattle Art Museum, *Manuel Neri*, January 15–March 1. Catalogue
        Charles Cowles Gallery, New York, *Manuel Neri*, February 7–28. Brochure
        The Mexican Museum, San Francisco, *Manuel Neri: Sculpture/Drawings*, May 7–June 5
        The Art Museum Association, *Manuel Neri: Drawings and Bronzes*. Travel through 1983 to: Redding Museum and Art Center, Redding, CA; Fresno Art Center, Fresno, CA; Gardiner State University Art Gallery, Stillwater, OK; San Jose Museum of Art, San Jose, CA; North Dakota State University, Fargo; Arkansas Art Center, Little Rock; Abilene Fine Arts Museum, Abilene, TX; Art Museum of Santa Cruz County, Santa Cruz, CA; Florida International University, Miami; Springfield Art Museum, Springfield, MO; Honolulu Academy of Art; Laumeier International Sculpture Park, St. Louis, MO. Brochure
        John Berggruen Gallery, San Francisco, *Manuel Neri*, November 17–December 19
1982   Charles Cowles Gallery, New York, *Manuel Neri*, November 7–27
1983   Middendorf/Lane Gallery, Washington, DC, *Manuel Neri, Sculpture and Drawings*, January 26–February 22
1984   John Berggruen Gallery, San Francisco, *Manuel Neri, Sculpture and Drawings*, February 23–March 24
        Middendorf Gallery, Washington, DC, *Manuel Neri*, March 10–31
        Art Gallery, California State University, Chico, *The Human Figure: Sculpture and Drawings by Manuel Neri*, March 26–April 13
        Gimpel-Hanover + Andre Emmerich Galerien, Zurich, Switzerland, *Manuel Neri*, April 16–June 7
1985   Robert Else Gallery, California State University, Sacramento, *Manuel Neri: Sculpture and Drawings*, October 15–November 12. Catalogue
1986   Charles Cowles Gallery, New York, *Manuel Neri*, February 1–March 1
1987   Fay Gold Gallery, Atlanta, *Manuel Neri: Sculpture and Drawings*, March 14–April 22
        San Antonio Art Institute, San Antonio, TX, *Manuel Neri*, November 24–December 22

1988   College of Notre Dame, Belmont, CA, *Manuel Neri, A Personal Selection*, April 14–May 21. Brochure
        John Berggruen Gallery, San Francisco, *Manuel Neri: Recent Sculpture and Drawings*, April 28–May 28
        James Corcoran Gallery, Santa Monica, CA, October 29–November 27
1989   Sheppard Gallery, University of Nevada, Reno, March 10–April 3
        Charles Cowles Gallery, New York, *Manuel Neri, New Works: Marble and Plaster*, April 29–May 27
        San Francisco Museum of Modern Art, *Manuel Neri: Plaster*, May 25–July 23. Catalogue
        Greg Kucera Gallery, Seattle, *Manuel Neri: Sculpture and Drawings*, June 1–July 9
        Riva Yares Gallery, Scottsdale, AZ, *Manuel Neri: Sculpture of the 1980s*, November 18–December 25. Catalogue
1990   John Berggruen Gallery, San Francisco, *Manuel Neri*, March 21–April 21
        Crocker Art Museum, Sacramento, CA, *Manuel Neri: Bronzes*, August 10–October 21. Catalogue
        Bingham Kurts Gallery, Memphis, TN, *Manuel Neri: Works on Paper*, October 19–November 13
        Dominican College, San Rafael, CA, November 15–December 15
        Margulies/Taplin Gallery, Coconut Grove, FL, *Manuel Neri*, December 28, 1990–January 23, 1991
1991   Charles Cowles Gallery, New York, *Manuel Neri*, February 2–23
        Richard L. Nelson Gallery, University of California, Davis, *Manuel Neri: Drawings, Part I, 1953–1974*, April 7–May 19
        Eve Mannes Gallery, Atlanta, *Manuel Neri*, April 12–June 15
        Riva Yares Gallery, Santa Fe, NM, *Manuel Neri*, June 1–August 31
1992   John Berggruen Gallery, San Francisco, *Manuel Neri*, March 5–April 4
        Morgan Gallery, Kansas City, MO, *Manuel Neri*, March 27–May 2
        Margulies/Taplin Gallery, Boca Raton, FL, May 7–June 11
        Fresno Art Center, Fresno, CA, *She Said: I Tell You It Doesn't Hurt Me*, June 5–August 16
1993   Bingham Kurts Gallery, Memphis, TN, *Manuel Neri*, January 8–31
        Charles Cowles Gallery, New York, *Manuel Neri, New Work: Marbles, Bronzes and Works on Paper*, January 28–March 6
        Riva Yares Gallery, Scottsdale, AZ, *Manuel Neri*, February 11–March 9
        University of Alabama Art Gallery, Tuscaloosa, *Manuel Neri: Drawings and Sculpture*, March 26–May 2
        Dia Center for the Arts, Bridgehampton, NY, *Manuel Neri: Painted and Unpainted*, July 31–September 19. Catalogue
        Campbell-Thiebaud Gallery, San Francisco, *Manuel Neri*, August 31–October 2. Catalogue
1994   Margulies/Taplin Gallery, Boca Raton, FL, February 2–23
        Hearst Art Gallery, St. Mary's College, Moraga, CA, *Manuel Neri: Master Artist Tribute III*, November 11–December 23

GROUP EXHIBITIONS

1955   The 6 Gallery, San Francisco
        Oakland Annual, Oakland, CA
1957   Richmond Art Center, Richmond, CA
        The 6 Gallery, San Francisco
        Oakland Annual, Oakland, CA
1958   San Francisco Art Annual, San Francisco
        Berkeley Gallery, Berkeley, CA
1959   San Francisco Museum of Art, *Paintings by Sam Francis, Wally Hedrick, and Fred Martin, Sculpture by Wally Hedrick and Manuel Neri*, February 3–22
1960   Batman Gallery, San Francisco, *Group Show*, December
1961   Staempfli Gallery, New York
        California Palace of the Legion of Honor, San Francisco, *The Nude*, September

1962   Stanford University Art Gallery, Stanford, CA, *Some Points of View—'62*, October 30–November 20. Catalogue
        Houston Contemporary Arts Museum, *San Francisco 9*
        Primus-Stuart Gallery, Los Angeles
        San Francisco Art Institute, *Works in Clay*
        Staempfli Gallery, New York
1963   San Francisco Art Institute, *Some New Art in the Bay Area*, March–April
        The Oakland Museum, Oakland, CA, *California Sculpture Today*, August 4–September 15
        Kaiser Center, Oakland, CA, *California Sculpture Today*
        San Francisco Art Institute, *82nd Annual Invitational*
        Primus-Stuart Gallery, Los Angeles
1964   Stanford University Art Museum, Stanford, CA, *Current Painting and Sculpture of the Bay Area*, October 8–November 29. Catalogue
        David Stuart Gallery, Los Angeles, *Joan Brown/Manuel Neri*
1965   San Francisco Museum of Art, *Bay Region: Prints and Drawings* (Two-artist show with Wayne Thiebaud), January 12–February 21
1966   University of California, Irvine, *Abstract Expressionist Ceramics*. Travel to the San Francisco Museum of Art
        Berkeley Gallery, San Francisco, *The Slant Step Show*, September
1967   University Art Museum, Berkeley, CA, *Funk Art*, April 18–May 29
        California State College, Fullerton, *Recorded Images/Dimensional Media*, October 20–November 12
1968   Portland Art Museum, Portland, OR, *The West Coast Now*, February 9–March 6. Travel to San Francisco and Los Angeles
        San Francisco Museum of Art, *On Looking Back: Bay Area, 1945–1962*, August 8–September 8
        University of Nevada, Reno, *Sculpture Invitational*. Catalogue
1969   Berkeley Gallery, San Francisco, *The Repair Show*, March 13–April 4
        Worth Ryder Gallery, University of California, Berkeley, *Visiting Artists: Leonard Edmondson, Joseph Raffael, Manuel Neri*, August 8–31
        Jason Aver Gallery, San Francisco, *Four Man Show: Tony DeLap, Craig Kauffman, Ed Moses, Manuel Neri*, December
        Reed College, Portland, OR, *Six Bay Area Artists*
1970   Memorial Union Gallery, University of California, Davis, *Garden Show*, January
        University Art Museum, Berkeley, CA, *The Eighties*, March 17–April 12
        San Francisco Art Institute, *Manuel Neri and William Geis*, September–October
        Whitney Museum of American Art, New York, *Annual Exhibition: Contemporary American Sculpture*
1971   The Oakland Museum, Oakland, CA, *Sculptured Lines* (with Harold Paris and Gerald Walburg), July 27–September 5
        University of Nevada, Reno, *Manuel Neri and William Wiley*, October
        St. Mary's College Art Gallery, Moraga, CA, *The Good Drawing Show*, October 30–November 26. Catalogue
        Quay Gallery, San Francisco, *Group Show*
1972   E. B. Crocker Art Gallery, Sacramento, CA, *Sacramento Sampler I*, April 1–May 7. Travel to The Oakland Museum, Oakland, CA, May 23–July 2
        Walnut Creek Civic Arts Gallery, Walnut Creek, CA, *It's for the Birds*, September 29–October 29
        Artists Contemporary Gallery, Sacramento, CA, *A Ladder Show*, October 6–31. Catalogue
        Quay Gallery, San Francisco, *Group Show*
1973   Palo Alto Cultural Center, Palo Alto, CA, *First Sculpture Invitational*, January 13–February 18
        St. Mary's College Art Gallery, Moraga, CA, *The Small Format*, September 1–28. Catalogue
        Nelson I. C. Gallery, University of California, Davis, *Manuel Neri, Cornelia Schulz, and Elyn Zimmerman*, October 1–26

San Francisco Art Institute, *Drawing Invitational*

1974   San Francisco Museum of Art, *A Third World Painting and Sculpture Exhibition*, June 8–July 28. Catalogue

Quay Gallery, San Francisco, *Group Show*, August

1975   The Oakland Museum, Oakland, CA, *Public Sculpture/Urban Environment*, September–December

University of California, Davis, *Department Faculty Exhibition*, April 2–29

Gallery Smith-Anderson, Palo Alto, CA, *Print Show*. Travel to Institute of Experimental Printmaking, Santa Cruz, CA, June–July

Helen Euphrat Gallery, De Anza College, Cupertino, CA, *A Survey of Sculptural Directions in the Bay Area*, October 3–30

Linda Farris Gallery, Seattle, *Images of Woman*, November

Hansen Fuller Gallery, San Francisco, *Hansen Fuller Gallery Pays Tribute to the San Francisco Art Institute* (Curated by Fred Martin), November–December. Catalogue

JPL Gallery, London, *Sculptors as Draughtsmen*

JPL Gallery, London, *California Gold* (Sponsored by the U.S. Information Agency), October 15–November 21. Travel through 1978 to museums and galleries in Europe, the Middle East, and India. Catalogue

1976   James Willis Gallery, San Francisco, *Retrospective of Sculpture in the Bay Area*, January 23–March 12

Martha Jackson Gallery, New York, *Graphics from the International Institute of Experimental Printmaking*, February 12–March 6

San Francisco Museum of Modern Art, *California Painting and Sculpture: The Modern Era*, September 3, 1976–January 2, 1977. Travel to The National Collection of Fine Arts, Washington, DC, May 20–September 11, 1977. Catalogue

San Francisco Art Institute, *Other Sources: An American Essay*, September 17–November 7. Catalogue

Santa Barbara Museum of Art, Santa Barbara, CA, *The Handmade Paper Object*, October 29–November 29. Travel to The Oakland Museum, Oakland, CA, December 21, 1976–February 6, 1977; The Institute for Contemporary Art, Boston, May 10–June 14, 1977; The Johnson Museum at Cornell University, Ithaca, NY, July 6–August 14, 1977; Jacksonville Museum of Art, Jacksonville, FL, September 8–October 9, 1977. Catalogue

Braunstein/Quay Gallery, San Francisco, *New Work: Bruce Conner and Manuel Neri*, November 2–27

Art Gallery of New South Wales, Sydney, Australia, *The Biennale of Sydney*, November 11–December 19. Catalogue

1977   Diablo Valley College Art Gallery, Diablo Valley, CA, *Artist's Studio Floor Sweeping Show*, March 2–30

Braunstein/Quay Gallery, New York, *Works on Paper*, March 8–April 2

Huntsville Museum of Art, Huntsville, AL, *California Bay Area Art—Update*, May 6–June 15. Catalogue

Kenmin Prefecture Hall, Tokyo, *Tokyo/Bay Area Exchange of Contemporary Art: Kenmin Prefecture Hall, Tokyo/80 Langton Street, San Francisco*, October 25–November 12

Santa Rosa Junior College Art Gallery, Santa Rosa, CA, *Contemporary Figurative Sculpture*, November 6–14

Lang Art Gallery, Scripps College, Claremont, CA, *Paper Art*, November 9–December 21

Center for the Visual Arts, Oakland, CA, *Sculpture Show*, November 19–December 15

Smithsonian Institution Traveling Exhibition Service, Washington, DC, *Paper as Medium*. Catalogue

Braunstein/Quay Gallery, San Francisco, *Gallery Group Show*

Weatherspoon Art Gallery, University of North Carolina, Greensboro

1978   University of New Mexico Art Museum, Albuquerque, *Bay Area Art of the 60's and 70's, The Gift of Dr. Sam West*, January 8–March 19. Catalogue

Gallery Paule Anglim, San Francisco, January

Sonoma State College, Rohnert Park, CA, *Northern California Artists*, April 7–May 5

Hayward Area Festival of the Arts, Hayward, CA, *17th Annual Hayward Festival of the Arts—Invitational Exhibit*, May 19–21. Catalogue

Everson Museum of Art, Syracuse, NY, *A Century of Ceramics in the United States 1878–1978*. Catalogue

1979   Hansen Fuller Gallery, San Francisco, *Related Figurative Drawings*, January

Gallery Paule Anglim, San Francisco, *Manuel Neri, Jay De Feo, Hassel Smith, Nathan Oliveira, Philip Guston*, January 6–February 3

Central Washington State College, Ellensburg, *Annual Drawing Invitational* (Curated by Elmer Bischoff), February

Civic Arts Gallery, Walnut Creek, CA, *Humanform*

Independent Curators, New York, *Masks*. Travel in U.S. through 1981

The Oakland Museum, Oakland, CA, *10" × 10"*

1980   Gallery Paule Anglim, San Francisco, *Manuel Neri and Hassel Smith: Drawings*, March

San Diego Museum of Art, San Diego, CA, *Sculpture in California 1975–1980*, May 9–June 22

International Sculpture Center, Washington, DC, *The Eleventh International Sculpture Conference Exhibition*, June

Nassau County Museum of Fine Art, Roslyn, NY, *Contemporary Naturalism: Works of the 1970s*, June 8–August 24. Catalogue

San Francisco Museum of Modern Art, *20 American Artists*, July 24–September 7. Catalogue

Palo Alto Cultural Center, Palo Alto, CA, *Painted Sculpture*, August 31–October 26

Santa Rosa Junior College Art Gallery, Santa Rosa, CA

The Mexican Museum, San Francisco, *Los Primeros Cinco Años/Fifth Anniversary Exhibit*, November 20, 1980–January 11, 1981. Brochure

1981   John Berggruen Gallery, San Francisco, *Salute to the San Francisco Art Institute: Elmer Bischoff, Ron Davis, Richard Diebenkorn, Manuel Neri, Nathan Oliveira, Wayne Thiebaud*, January

Triton Museum of Art, Santa Clara, CA, *San Francisco Alumni Exhibition*, January 9–March 9

Gallery Paule Anglim, San Francisco, *A View from 1959 San Francisco Museum of Modern Art: Sam Francis Selects Wally Hedrick, Fred Martin, Manuel Neri, Sam Francis*, January 10–February 14

California College of Arts and Crafts, Oakland, CA, *California College of Arts and Crafts Alumni Exhibition*, January 15–February 10

Sierra Nevada Museum of Art, Reno, NV, *Davis School: Prints and Drawings*, January 24–February 22

Civic Arts Gallery, Walnut Creek, CA, *"Remember It's Only Art": From the Collection of the San Francisco Museum of Modern Art*, February 5–March 28. Catalogue

Provincetown Art Association and Museum, Provincetown, MA, *The Sun Gallery*, July 24–August 30. Catalogue

Middendorf/Lane Gallery, Washington, DC, *The Figure in Bronze: Small Scale*, October 13–November 17

Tulane University, New Orleans, *Variants: Drawings by Sculptors*, October 15, 1981–May 30, 1982

Quay Gallery, San Francisco, *Sculptors' Work on Paper*, November 3–28

American Academy and Institute of Arts and Letters, New York, *Hassam Fund Purchase Exhibit*, November 16–December 20

1982   John Berggruen Gallery, San Francisco, *Recent Works*, February 17–March 24. Catalogue

American Academy and Institute of Arts and Letters, New York, *Paintings and Sculpture by Candidates for Art Awards*, March 8–April 4

Studio Nine, Benicia, CA, *Benicia Sculptors*, March 27–April 16

Okun-Thomas Gallery, St. Louis, MO, April

Dart Gallery, Chicago, *Non-Objective Sculpture*, April 10–May 4

The Mexican Museum, San Francisco, *Cinco de Mayo Inaugural Exhibit at Fort Mason Center*, May 5–July 3. Brochure

American Academy and Institute of Arts and Letters, New York, *Paintings and Sculptures by Recipients of Art Awards*, May 19–June 13

University Art Museum, Berkeley, CA, *Bay Area Sculpture from the Collection*, Summer

TransAmerica Pyramid, San Francisco, *Survey of Bay Area Figurative Sculptors*, July 8–August 16

Fuller Goldeen Gallery, San Francisco, *Casting: A Survey of Cast Metal Sculpture in the 80's*, July 8–August 28

John Berggruen Gallery, San Francisco, *Aspects of Sculpture*, August 4–September 4

Claremont Hotel, Berkeley, CA, *Project Sculpture*, August 4–October 31. Catalogue

The Oakland Museum, Oakland, CA, *100 Years of Sculpture*, August 7–October 17. Catalogue

Kaiser Center, Oakland, CA, *The Brook House Sculpture Invitational at the Kaiser Center*, August 8, 1982–January 19, 1983. Catalogue

Fresno Arts Center, Fresno, CA, *Forgotten Dimension: A Survey of Small Sculpture in California Now*. Traveled by the Art Museum Association to San Francisco International Airport, August 6–September 17; Center for the Visual Arts, Illinois State University, Normal, October 11–November 22; Aspen Center for the Visual Arts, Aspen, CO, December 10, 1982–January 20, 1983; Florida International University, Miami, February 10–March 24, 1983; Laumeier International Sculpture Park, St. Louis, MO, April 14–June 2, 1983; Mary and Leigh Block Gallery, Northwestern University, Evanston, IL, July 27–September 11, 1983; Colorado Gallery of the Arts, Littleton, October 6–November 24, 1983. Catalogue

Richard L. Nelson Gallery, Memorial Union Art Gallery, and Pence Gallery, University of California, Davis, *Sculptors at UC Davis: Past & Present*, September 20–October 29. Catalogue

DeSaisset Museum, University of Santa Clara, Santa Clara, CA, *Northern California Art of the Sixties*, October 12–December 12. Catalogue

1983   San Francisco Museum of Modern Art, *Resource/Reservoir, CCAC: 75 Years*, January 13–February 27. Brochure

Sarah Lawrence Gallery, Sarah Lawrence College, Bronxville, NY, *The United States of the Arts*, February 1–March 13. Brochure

Seattle Art Museum, *Recent West Coast Acquisitions*, February 12–April 26

Glastonbury Gallery, San Francisco, *A Selection of Contemporary Drawings*, February 17–March 31

John Berggruen Gallery, San Francisco, *Selected Sculpture*, March 23–April 2

Frumkin-Struve Gallery, Chicago, *Bronze Sculpture*, March 25–April 30

San Francisco Museum of Modern Art, *Selections from the Permanent Collection/Sculpture*, April–June 5

San Francisco Museum of Modern Art, *Bay Area Collects*, April 21–June 26

Monterey Peninsula Museum of Art, Monterey, CA, *California Contemporary: Recent Work of Twenty-three Artists*, May 1–29. Catalogue

Museum of Anthropology, California State University, Hayward, *Sons of the Shaking Earth*, May 2–June 10. Brochure

Renaissance Society, University of Chicago, *The Sixth Day*, May 8–June 15. Catalogue

Michael Himovitz Gallery, Carmichael, CA, *Continuum*, September–October 5

Institute of Contemporary Art of the Virginia Museum, Richmond, *Sculpture Now: Recent Figurative Works*, October 11–November 13

1984   Spokane Center Gallery, Eastern Washington University, Cheney, *Figurative Bronze Sculpture*, January 13–February 23

Richard L. Nelson Gallery, University of California, Davis, *Painters at UC Davis, Part I: 1950s–1960s*, January 23–February 21

Stephen Wirtz Gallery, San Francisco, *Artist's Call*, February

California State University, Long Beach, *Figurative Sculpture: Ten Artists/Two Decades*, March 13–April 29. Catalogue

Hirshhorn Museum and Sculpture Garden, Washington, DC, *Drawings Since 1974*, March 15–May 13. Catalogue

Gille Mansillon Gallery, Santa Monica, CA, *Twelve Californian Artists*, May

The Mexican Museum, San Francisco, *Spectrum: A View of Mexican American Art*, May 2–September 30

Charles Cowles Gallery, Venice, CA, June–July

Fisher Gallery, University of Southern California, Los Angeles, *California Sculpture Show* (Organized by California/International Arts Foundation), June 2–August 12. Travel to: CAPC (Musée d'Art Contemporain de Bordeaux), Bordeaux, France, October 5–December 12; Stadtische Kunsthalle, Mannheim, West Germany, February–April 1985; Yorkshire Sculpture Park, West Bretton, England, May 1985; Sonja Henies og Neils Onstads Stiftelser, Hovikodden (Oslo), Norway, September 1985. Catalogue

Gille Mansillon Gallery, Santa Monica, CA, *SF-LA*, June 21–July 27

Richard L. Nelson Gallery, University of California, Davis, *Juxtapositions*, September 12–October 26

Concourse Gallery, Bank of America World Headquarters, San Francisco, *Highlights: Selections from the BankAmerica Corporate Art Collection*, October 11–November 27

The Oakland Museum, Oakland, CA, *Dilexi Years*, October 13–December 16

Art Gallery, Sonoma State University, Rohnert Park, CA, *Works in Bronze, A Modern Survey*, November 2–December 16. Travel through 1986. Catalogue

Seattle Art Museum, *American Sculpture: Three Decades*, November 15, 1984–January 27, 1985

American Academy and Institute of Arts and Letters, New York, *36th Annual Purchase Exhibition: Hassam and Speicher Fund*, November 19–December 16. Brochure

San Francisco Museum of Modern Art, *The 20th Century: The San Francisco Museum of Modern Art Collection*, December 9, 1984–February 17, 1985. Catalogue

1985   John Berggruen Gallery, San Francisco, *Recent Acquisitions*, January 9–February 2

Santa Barbara Museum of Art, Santa Barbara, CA, *Santa Barbara Collects, Part I*, January 26–March 24. Catalogue

John Berggruen Gallery, San Francisco, *Group Exhibition*, March 13–April 6

Gallery One, Fort Worth, TX, *Drawings: Coast to Coast*, April 27–June 1

The Oakland Museum, Oakland, CA, *Art in the San Francisco Bay Area, 1945–1980*, June 15–August 18

Concourse Gallery, Bank of America World Headquarters, San Francisco, *M. Lee Fatherree: Photographs of Artists*, August 1–October 1

The Contemporary Arts Center, Cincinnati, OH, *Body & Soul: Aspects of Recent Figurative Sculpture*, September 5–October 12. Travel to Knight Gallery, Charlotte, NC, February 1–March 30, 1986; Fresno Arts Center, Fresno, CA, May 3–June 28, 1986; Loch Haven Art Center, Orlando, FL, August 17–October 12, 1986; Visual Arts Gallery, Florida International University, Miami, October 24–December 1, 1986; Joslyn Art Museum, Omaha, NE, January 31–March 28, 1987; Jacksonville Art Museum, Jacksonville, FL, May 2–June 27, 1987. Catalogue

San Francisco Museum of Modern Art, *American Realism: Twentieth-Century Drawings and Watercolors from the Glenn C. Janss Collection*, November 7, 1985–January 12, 1986. Travel to De Cordova and Dana Museum, Lincoln, MA, February 13–April 6, 1986;

Huntington Art Gallery, University of Texas, Austin, July 31–
September 21, 1986; Mary and Leigh Block Gallery, Northwestern
University, Evanston, IL, October 23–December 14, 1986; Williams
College Museum of Art, Williamstown, MA, January 15–March
1987; Akron Art Museum, Akron, OH, April 9–May 31, 1987;
Madison Art Center, Madison, WI, July 2–September 20, 1987.
Catalogue

Sheldon Memorial Art Gallery, University of Nebraska, Lincoln,
Contemporary Bronze: Six in the Figurative Tradition, November
19, 1985–January 19, 1986. Travel to Kansas City Art Institute,
Kansas City, KS, February 11–March 23, 1986; Des Moines Art
Center, Des Moines, IA, April 8–May 13, 1986. Catalogue

1986   John Berggruen Gallery, San Francisco, *Selected Works by 20th
Century Masters,* January 15–February 8

University Art Museum, Berkeley, CA, *Cal Collects,* April 2–May 18.
Brochure

Kaufman Astoria Studios, Astoria, NY, *Human Form from the Media
Age,* May 1–July 15

909 Third Avenue and The Mendik Company, New York, *Universal
Images: People and Nature in Sculpture,* May 21–September 5

Marilyn Pearl Gallery, New York, *Figurative Sculpture: The 80's,*
June 10–July 3

San Francisco Museum of Modern Art, *California Sculpture:
1959–1980,* July 20–August 24

John Berggruen Gallery, San Francisco, *Selected Acquisitions,*
September 10–October 11

Carl Schlosberg Fine Arts, Sherman Oaks, CA, *Contemporary
Figurative Sculpture,* September 28–October 31

Center for the Arts, Vero Beach, FL, *Collectors' Choice,* October
1986–February 1987

John Berggruen Gallery, Monadnock Building, San Francisco,
Sculpture and Works in Relief, October 9–November 29

North Dakota Museum of Art, Grand Forks, *Casting Across America:
An Artist Selects,* October 10–November 9

Pacific Bell, San Ramon, CA, *The Contemporary Bay Area Figurative
School* (Organized by Fine Arts Services, Inc., Los Angeles),
November 24–December 19

1987   Charles Cowles Gallery, New York, *New Works,* January 17–
February 21

Palm Springs Desert Museum, Palm Springs, CA, *California Figurative
Sculpture,* January 30–March 15. Catalogue

John Berggruen Gallery, Monadnock Building, San Francisco, *New
Acquisitions,* January 27–March 28

Foster/White Gallery, Seattle, *National Sculpture Exhibition, 1987,*
February 5–March 1

The Art Store Gallery, San Francisco, *Sculpture and Paint,* March 26–
April 23

Sheppard Fine Arts Gallery, University of Nevada, Reno, *30 From 25,*
April 24–May 22. Catalogue

Museum of Fine Arts, Houston, *Contemporary Hispanic Art in the
United States,* May 2–July 26. Travel to Corcoran Gallery of Art,
Washington, DC; Brooklyn Museum, Brooklyn, NY; Museum of
Fine Arts and Museum of International Folk Art, Santa Fe, NM;
Denver Art Museum; Los Angeles County Museum of Art.
Catalogue

John Berggruen Gallery, Monadnock Building, San Francisco, *New
Acquisitions,* May–June

Richmond Art Center, Richmond, CA, *Bay Area Drawing,* May 15–
July 16

Charles Cowles Gallery, New York, *Summer Exhibition Space, 1987,*
Summer

871 Fine Arts, San Francisco, *The Triumph of the Figure in Bay Area
Art: 1950–1965,* September 5–December 31. Brochure

Philbrook Art Center, Tulsa, OK, *The Eloquent Object,* September 20,
1987–January 3, 1988. Travel to The Oakland Museum, Oakland,
CA, February 20–May 15, 1988. Catalogue

Art Gallery, University of Nebraska, Lincoln, *Sculptors' Works on
Paper,* September 28–October 14

San Francisco International Airport, *The Right Foot Show,* October 5,
1987–January 15, 1988

Davis Art Center, Davis, CA, *Three Decades of Davis Art,*
November 13–December 20

American Academy and Institute of Arts and Letters, New York, *39th
Annual Academy-Institute Purchase Exhibition,* November 16–
December 13

Madison Art Center, Madison, WI, *Sculptors on Paper: New Work,*
December 5, 1987–January 31, 1988. Travel to Pittsburgh Center
for the Arts, Pittsburgh, PA; Kalamazoo Institute of Arts,
Kalamazoo, MI; Sheldon Memorial Art Gallery, Lincoln, NE.
Catalogue

Charles Cowles Gallery, New York, *New Works by Gallery Artists,*
December 5, 1987–January 9, 1988

1988   Walnut Creek Civic Arts Gallery, Walnut Creek, CA, *Bay Area
Bronze,* January 13–March 12

John Berggruen Gallery, Monadnock Building, San Francisco,
Selected Sculpture, January 16–February 27

John Berggruen Gallery, San Francisco, *Works on Paper,* January 19–
February 20

Gallery Camino Real, Boca Raton, FL, *The Figurative Image Today,*
January 29–March 1

Art Gallery, Santa Rosa Junior College, Santa Rosa, CA, *Drawing,*
February 2–March 2

Palo Alto Cultural Center, Palo Alto, CA, *Bay Area Sculpture: Metal,
Stone and Wood,* February 21–April 24

Memorial Union Gallery, University of California, Davis, *Bronze
Works: Northern California Artists,* February 28–April 17

Pine Street Lobby Gallery, Gerald D. Hines Inc., San Francisco,
The Downtown Foot Show, February 29–May 5. Brochure

John Berggruen Gallery, San Francisco; *Selected Paintings and
Sculpture,* March 23–April 23

Natsoulas/Novelozo Gallery, Davis, CA, *30 Ceramic Sculptors,*
April 8–May 10. Catalogue

Mendocino Arts Center, Mendocino, CA, *In Relief: Works of Cast
Paper,* June 14–July 24

Eve Mannes Gallery, Atlanta, *Top Choices,* July 8–August 31

Sierra Nevada Museum of Art, Reno, NV, *West Coast Contemporary,*
July 14–August 14

James Corcoran Gallery, Santa Monica, CA, *Lost and Found in California: Four Decades of Assemblage Art,* July 16–September 7. Catalogue

Natsoulas/Novelozo Gallery, Davis, CA, *New Work '88,* August 12–
October 1

John Berggruen Gallery, San Francisco, *Works on Paper,* September 8–
October 8. Catalogue

The Bronx Museum of the Arts, Bronx, NY, *The Latin American
Spirit: Art and Artists in the United States, 1920–1970,* September
29, 1988–January 27, 1989. Travel to El Paso Museum of Art,
El Paso, TX, February 27–April 23, 1989; San Diego Museum of
Art, San Diego, CA, May 22–July 16, 1989; Instituto de Cultura
Puertorriqueña, San Juan, PR, August 14–October 8, 1989;
Center for the Arts, Vero Beach, FL, January 28–March 31, 1990.
Catalogue

Leavenworth Carnegie Arts Center, Leavenworth, KS, *Contemporary
Masters Kansas Tour: Selections from the Collection of South-
western Bell Corporation,* November 4–December 26. Travel to
Baker Arts Center, Liberal, KS, January 5–February 12, 1989;
Edwin A. Ulrich Museum of Art, Wichita State University,
Wichita, KS, April 5–30, 1989; Salina Arts Center, Salina, KS,

June 5–July 21, 1989; Norman R. Eppink Art Gallery, Emporia State University, Emporia, KS, July 31–October 1, 1989; Mulvane Art Museum, Washburn University, Topeka, KS, October 8–31, 1989. Catalogue

Carl Schlosberg Fine Art, Sherman Oaks, CA, *Sculpture: Works in Bronze*, November 6–27

Weatherspoon Art Gallery, University of North Carolina, Greensboro, *Art on Paper*, November 13–December 11

Sheehan Gallery, Whitman College, Walla Walla, WA, *Cast in Walla Walla*, November 14–December 16

Art Department Gallery, San Francisco State University, *Counter Visions: Pioneers in Bay Area Art*, November 16–December 9. Brochure

1989 Charles Cowles Gallery, New York, *The Cowles Art Show*, February 4–25

San Francisco International Airport, *California Artists Who Are Educators*, February 13–March 30

Walnut Creek Civic Arts Gallery, Walnut Creek, CA, *The Benicia Studio Community*, February 18–March 25

California Museum of Science and Industry, Los Angeles, *Marmo: The New Italian Stone Age*, March 16–April 30. Catalogue

Natsoulas/Novelozo Gallery, Davis, CA, *30 Ceramic Sculptors*, April 7–May 6. Catalogue

Richard L. Nelson Gallery, University of California, Davis, *A.C.D.H.H.H.J.N.P.P.S.T.*, April 23–May 24

John Berggruen Gallery, Monadnock Building, San Francisco, *Sculpture*, July 19–September 2

Security Pacific Gallery, Los Angeles, *Sculptural Intimacies: Recent Small-Scale Work*, November 12, 1989–January 6, 1990. Catalogue

San Francisco Museum of Modern Art, *Bay Area Figurative Art: 1950–1965*, December 14, 1989–February 4, 1990. Travel to Hirshhorn Museum and Sculpture Garden, Washington, DC, June 13–September 9, 1990; Pennsylvania Academy of the Fine Arts, Philadelphia, October 15–December 30, 1990. Catalogue

1990 Natsoulas/Novelozo Gallery, Davis, CA, *Lyrical Vision: The '6' Gallery, 1954–1957*, January 12–February 23. Catalogue

Arkansas Art Center, Little Rock, *National Drawing Invitational*, March 1–April 8

Natsoulas/Novelozo Gallery, Davis, CA, *30 Ceramic Sculptors*, April 6–May 3. Catalogue

Campbell-Thiebaud Gallery, San Francisco, *Works on Paper*, May 1–June 2

Charles Cowles Gallery, New York, *Newer Sculpture*, June 1–29

Barbara Kornblatt Gallery, Washington, DC, *Manuel Neri, Erik Levine, Mel Chin*, June 5–July 28

Braunstein/Quay Gallery, San Francisco, *Bay Area Sculpture of the '60's, Past to Present*, June 7–July 7

Queens Museum, Queens, NY, *The Expressionist Surface: Contemporary Art in Plaster*, June 9–August 1

Butler Institute, Youngstown, OH, *California A–Z and Return*, June 24–August 19

The Mexican Museum, San Francisco, *From Folk to Fine: Fifteenth Anniversary Celebration*, December 7, 1990–April 31, 1991

1991 John Berggruen Gallery, San Francisco, *Large Scale Works on Paper*, February 21–March 16

Larry Evans Fine Art, The Rucker Fuller Company, San Francisco, *A Group Show of Bay Area Artists*, March–April

Carl Schlosberg Fine Arts, Malibu, CA, *Malibu in June*, June 1–29

Eve Mannes Gallery, Atlanta, *Top Choices*, June 15–August

John Berggruen Gallery, San Francisco, *Small Format Works on Paper*, June 26–August 3

Charles Cowles Gallery, New York, *Summer Group*, July 1–31

Anne Reed Gallery, Ketchum, ID, *Sculpture: Visions Transformed III*, July 5–August 9

John Berggruen Gallery, San Francisco, *Selected Sculpture*, August 7–28

The Fine Arts Museums of San Francisco, M. H. de Young Memorial Museum, *New Acquisitions*, September 11–November 17

Muckenthaler Cultural Center, Fullerton, CA, *Sculptural Perspectives for the Nineties*, October 6–December 29

Museo Estudio Diego Rivera, Mexico City, *Pasión por Frida*, October 11, 1991–January 31, 1992. Travel. Catalogue

Campbell-Thiebaud Gallery, San Francisco, *Twenty-five Treasures*, October 15–November 23

Tavelli Gallery, Aspen, CO, *Figures*, December 19, 1991–February 1, 1992

1992 Colorado University Art Galleries, Boulder, *20th Anniversary of the Visiting Artist Program*, January 17–February 15

Aspen Art Museum, Aspen, CO, *California North and South*, February 13–April 15

Hearst Art Gallery, St. Mary's College, Moraga, CA, *The Crucifixion Through the Modern Eye*, March 7–April 27

Carl Schlosberg Fine Arts, Sherman Oaks, CA, *George Rickey— Honoring 85 Years*, April 5–May 5

Margulies/Taplin Gallery, Boca Raton, FL, May 7–June 11

Whitney Museum of American Art, New York, *Gifts and Acquisitions in Context*, May 21–July 5

I. Wolk Gallery, St. Helena, CA, *"23"—23 Artists from John Berggruen Gallery*, June 22–July 24

Anne Reed Gallery, Ketchum, ID, *Visions Transformed IV*, July 8–August 5

John Berggruen Gallery, San Francisco, *Sculpture*, July 11–August 29

Syntex Corporation, Palo Alto, CA, *Bay Area Greats*, September 18–November 4

1993 One Market Plaza, San Francisco, *Revolution—Into the 2nd Century at San Francisco Art Institute*, January 4–March 26

Greg Kucera Gallery, Seattle, *Walla Walla Foundry: Selected Sculpture*, January 7–February 28

Anne Reed Gallery, Ketchum, ID, March 5–April 15

The Albuquerque Museum, Albuquerque, NM, *The Human Factor: Figurative Sculpture Reconsidered*, March 14–July 4

Newport Harbor Art Museum, Newport Beach, CA, *Beyond the Bay: The Figure*, May 12–June 27

Marriott Hotel, San Francisco, *Ventriloquist* (Exhibition accompanying the 40th Assembly of the American Psychiatric Association), May 21–26. Catalogue

Eve Mannes Gallery, Atlanta, *Group Show of Gallery Artists*, July–August

The Art Museum at Santa Cruz, Santa Cruz, CA, *Now and Again: Figure and Landscape*, October 2–November 21

Laguna Gloria Museum, Austin, TX, *Human Nature—Human Form*, October 30–December 12. Brochure

American Academy of Arts and Letters, New York, *45th Annual Academy Purchase Exhibition*, November 8–December 5

1994 Palo Alto Cultural Center, Palo Alto, CA, *Lyricism & Light*, January 20–April 24. Brochure

TransAmerica Pyramid Lobby Gallery, San Francisco, *The Figure in Sculpture*, February 2–April 13

Frumkin/Adams Gallery, New York, *California in the '70s: Bay Area Painting and Sculpture Revisited*, March 2–30

The Oakland Museum, Oakland, CA, *Here and Now: Bay Area Masterworks from the Di Rosa Collection*, March 11–May 8. Catalogue

Grounds for Sculpture, Hamilton, NJ, *Spring/Summer Exhibition*, May 21–September 30

Newport Harbor Art Museum, Newport Beach, CA, *The Essential Gesture*, October 15–December 31

BIBLIOGRAPHY

BOOKS

Albright, Thomas. *Art in the San Francisco Bay Area, 1945–1980.* Berkeley: University of California Press, 1985.

Andersen, Wayne. *American Sculpture in Process: 1930–1970.* Boston: New York Graphic Society, 1975.

Cancel, Luis R., et al. *The Latin American Spirit: Art and Artists in the United States, 1920–1970.* Bronx, NY: Bronx Museum of the Arts and Harry N. Abrams, 1988.

Clark, Garth, and Hughto, Margie. *A Century of Ceramics in the United States, 1878–1978.* New York: E. P. Dutton in association with the Everson Museum of Art, 1979.

Gilbert, Rita. *Living with Art.* New York: Random House, 1985.

Hopkins, Henry. *50 West Coast Artists.* San Francisco: Chronicle Books, 1981.

Jones, Caroline A. *Bay Area Figurative Art: 1950–1965.* Berkeley: University of California Press, 1989.

Klimenko, Mary Julia. *She Said: I Tell You It Doesn't Hurt Me.* San Diego: Brighton Press, 1991. Handpainted etchings by Manuel Neri. Limited edition of 33.

———. *Territory.* San Diego: Brighton Press, 1993. Photolithograph illustrations by Manuel Neri with one original drawing. Limited edition of 55.

Krantz, Les. *American Artists: An Illustrated Survey of Leading Americans.* Chicago: The Krantz Company Publishers, 1985.

Manhart, Marcia, and Manhart, Tom, eds. *The Eloquent Object.* Tulsa, OK: The Philbrook Museum of Art, 1987.

Martin, Alvin. *American Realism: Twentieth-Century Drawings and Watercolors From the Glenn C. Janss Collection.* New York: Harry N. Abrams, Inc., 1985.

Paz, Octavio; Beardsley, John; and Livingston, Jane. *Hispanic Art in the United States.* New York: Abbeville Press, 1987.

Plagens, Peter. *Sunshine Muse.* New York: Praeger Publishers, 1974.

Quirarte, Jacinto. *Mexican American Artists.* Austin: University of Texas Press, 1973.

CATALOGUES

80 Langton Street. *80 Langton Street: Documentation of the First Year.* San Francisco: 80 Langton Street, 1976.

Adelphia Society. *A Bid for Human Rights.* San Francisco: Adelphia Society, 1988.

Albright, Thomas. *Manuel Neri.* San Francisco: John Berggruen Gallery; Santa Monica, CA: James Corcoran Gallery; New York: Charles Cowles Gallery, 1988.

Albuquerque Museum. *The Human Factor: Figurative Sculpture Reconsidered.* Albuquerque: The Albuquerque Museum, 1993.

Amnesty International. *Artists for Amnesty.* Davis, CA: Amnesty International, 1987.

Armstrong, Richard. *Sculpture in California 1975–80.* San Diego: San Diego Museum of Art, 1980.

The Artists Association, San Francisco Art Institute. *Art Bank 64/66.* San Francisco: San Francisco Art Institute, 1966.

Barilleaux, Rene Paul. *Sculptors on Paper: New Work.* Madison, WI: Madison Art Center, 1987.

Bates, Mary, and Moulton, Susan. *Works in Bronze: A Modern Survey.* Rohnert Park, CA: Sonoma State University, 1984.

Bischoff, David A. *Manuel Neri: Sculpture and Drawings.* Sacramento, CA: Robert Else Gallery, California State University, 1985.

Bledsoe, Jane K. *Figurative Sculpture: Ten Artists/Two Decades.* Long Beach: University Art Museum, California State University, 1984.

Bolomey, Roger. *Forgotten Dimension—A Survey of Small Sculpture in California Now.* Fresno, CA: Fresno Arts Center, 1982.

Boynton, James, ed. *San Francisco 9.* Houston: Houston Contemporary Arts Museum, 1962.

Braunstein Gallery. *Braunstein Gallery Twentieth Anniversary.* San Francisco: Braunstein Gallery, 1981.

Brook House/Victor Fischer Fine Arts. *The Brook House Sculpture Invitational at Kaiser Center.* Orinda, CA: Victor Fischer Fine Arts, 1982.

Bush, Martin. *Figures of Contemporary Sculpture 1970–1990: Images of Man.* Tokyo: Brain Trust, Inc., 1992.

Butterfield, Jan, and Wortz, Melinda. *California Sculpture Show.* Los Angeles: California/International Arts Foundation, 1984.

Butterfield & Butterfield. *Contemporary Paintings, Watercolors, Drawings and Sculpture.* San Francisco: Butterfield & Butterfield, 1988.

Byer, Robert H. *Sculptural Intimacies—Recent Small-Scale Sculpture.* Los Angeles: Security Pacific Corporation, 1989.

Campbell-Thiebaud Gallery. *Manuel Neri: Recent Work.* San Francisco: Campbell-Thiebaud Gallery, 1993.

Castellon, Rolando. *A Third World Painting and Sculpture Exhibition.* San Francisco: San Francisco Museum of Art, 1974.

Clisby, Roger, ed. *Sacramento Sampler I.* Sacramento, CA: E. B. Crocker Art Gallery, 1972.

Coplans, John. *Abstract Expressionist Ceramics.* Irvine: University of California, 1966.

Costello, Daniel W.; Earls-Solari, Bonnie; and Stankus, Michelene. *BankAmerica Corporation Art Program 1985.* San Francisco: BankAmerica Corporation, 1986.

Culler, George D. *Some Points of View—'62.* Stanford, CA: Stanford University Art Gallery, 1962.

DeGroot, George. *California Contemporary: Recent Work of Twenty-three Artists.* Monterey, CA: Monterey Peninsula Museum of Art, 1983.

Dickson, Joanne. *Manuel Neri Sculpture & Drawings.* Seattle: Seattle Art Museum, 1981.

E. B. Crocker Art Gallery. *Manuel Neri: Recent Sculpture and Drawings.* Sacramento, CA: E. B. Crocker Art Gallery, 1977.

FitzGibbon, John. *California A–Z and Return.* Youngstown, OH: The Butler Institute of American Art, 1990.

Flood, Richard. *The Sixth Day.* Chicago: The Renaissance Society at the University of Chicago, 1983.

Foley, Suzanne. *Remember: It's Only Art.* Walnut Creek, CA: Civic Arts Gallery, 1981.

Fuller Goldeen Gallery. *Casting: A Survey of Cast Metal Sculpture in the '80s.* San Francisco: Fuller Goldeen Gallery, 1982.

Garduño, Blanca, and Rodriguez, José Antonio. *Pasión por Frida.* Mexico City: Museo Estudio Diego Rivera, 1991–92.

Gettings, Frank. *Drawings 1974–1984.* Washington, DC: Hirshhorn Museum and Sculpture Garden, 1984.

Goodwin, Erin. *A Survey of Sculptural Directions of the Bay Area.* Cupertino, CA: De Anza College, 1975.

Hayward Area Festival of the Arts. *17th Annual Hayward Festival of the Arts.* Hayward, CA: Hayward Area Festival of the Arts, 1978.

Henning, Robert, Jr., et al. *Santa Barbara Collects.* Santa Barbara, CA: Santa Barbara Museum of Art, 1985.

Holland, Katherine Church. *The Art Collection.* San Francisco: Federal Reserve Bank of San Francisco, 1986.

John Berggruen Gallery. *John Berggruen Gallery.* San Francisco: John Berggruen Gallery, 1986.

———. *Sculpture and Works in Relief.* San Francisco: John Berggruen Gallery, 1986.

———. *John Berggruen Gallery: Works on Paper.* San Francisco: John Berggruen Gallery, 1988.

———. *Large Scale Works on Paper.* San Francisco: John Berggruen Gallery, 1991.

Jones, Caroline A. *Manuel Neri: Plasters.* San Francisco: San Francisco Museum of Modern Art, 1989.

J.P.L. Fine Arts. *California Gold.* London: J.P.L. Fine Arts, 1975.

Kagawa, Paul, et al. *Other Sources: An American Essay.* San Francisco: San Francisco Art Institute, 1976.

Kiechel, Vivian. *Contemporary Bronze: Six in the Figurative Tradition.* Lincoln: Sheldon Memorial Art Gallery, University of Nebraska, 1985.

Lagoria, Georgianna M., and Martin, Fred. *Northern California Art of the Sixties.* Santa Clara, CA: De Saisset Museum, University of Santa Clara, 1982.

LaPlante, John D., ed. *Some Points of View—1962.* Stanford, CA: Stanford University Art Gallery, 1962.

Linhares, Phil. *Here and Now: Bay Area Masterworks from the Di Rosa Collection.* Oakland, CA: The Oakland Museum, 1994.

Magloff, Joanna, ed. *Current Painting and Sculpture of the Bay Area.* Stanford, CA: Stanford University Art Museum, 1964.

Matilsky, Barbara C. *The Expressionist Surface: Contemporary Art in Plaster.* Queens, NY: Queens Museum, 1990.

McCormick, Jim. *30 from 25.* Reno: Sheppard Fine Arts Gallery, University of Nevada, 1986.

McCullough, Tom; Thomas, Daniel; and Nicholson, Harry. *Three Views on the 1976 Biennale—Recent International Forms in Art.* Sydney, Australia: Art Gallery of New South Wales, 1976.

Morris, Dan W. *National Drawing Invitational.* Little Rock: The Arkansas Art Center, 1990.

Muckenthaler Cultural Center. *Sculptural Perspectives for the Nineties.* Fullerton, CA: Muckenthaler Art Center, 1991.

Nassau County Museum of Fine Art. *Contemporary Naturalism: Works of the 1970's.* Roslyn, NY: Nassau County Museum of Fine Art, 1980.

Natsoulas/Novelozo Gallery, with foreword by John Allen Ryan. *Lyrical Vision: The '6' Gallery 1954–1957.* Davis, CA: Natsoulas/Novelozo Gallery Press, 1989.

———, with foreword by John Natsoulas. *30 Ceramic Sculptors.* Davis, CA: Natsoulas/Novelozo Gallery, 1989.

———, with foreword by John Natsoulas. *30 Ceramic Sculptors.* Davis, CA: Natsoulas/Novelozo Gallery, 1990.

Neubert, George. *Manuel Neri, Sculptor.* Oakland, CA: The Oakland Museum, 1976.

———. *Bay Area Sculptors of the 1960s: Then and Now.* San Francisco: Braunstein/Quay Gallery, 1990.

Nierengarten-Smith, Beej. *Laumeier Sculpture Park First Decade, 1976–1986.* St. Louis, MO: Laumeier Sculpture Park, 1986.

Novakov, Anna. "Funk Art: A San Francisco Phenomenon." In *Painters at UC Davis.* Davis: Richard L. Nelson Gallery, University of California, 1984.

Oakland Museum. *100 Years of California Sculpture.* Oakland, CA: The Oakland Museum, 1982.

Orr-Cahall, Christina, ed. *The Dilexi Years 1958–1970.* Oakland, CA: The Oakland Museum, 1984.

———. *The Art of California: Selected Works from the Collection of The Oakland Museum.* Oakland, CA: The Oakland Museum; San Francisco: Chronicle Books, 1984.

Project Sculpture. *Project Sculpture.* Oakland, CA: Project Sculpture, 1982.

Provincetown Art Association and Museum. *The Sun Gallery.* Provincetown, MA: Provincetown Art Association and Museum, 1981.

Rannells, Susan, and Richardson, Brenda. *Free.* Berkeley, CA: University Art Museum, 1970.

Restany, Pierre. *Manuel Neri.* San Francisco: John Berggruen Gallery; New York: Charles Cowles Gallery; Zurich: Gimpel-Hanover + Andre Emmerich Galerien, 1984.

Richard L. Nelson Gallery. *Sculptors at UC Davis: Past and Present.* Davis: Richard L. Nelson Gallery, University of California, 1972.

———. *Painters at UC Davis.* Davis: Richard L. Nelson Gallery, University of California, 1984.

Riva Yares Gallery. *Manuel Neri: Sculpture of the 1980s.* Scottsdale, AZ: Riva Yares Gallery, 1989.

Rodriguez, Peter. *The Mexican Museum.* San Francisco: The Mexican Museum, 1981.

Rogers-Lafferty, Sarah. *Body & Soul: Aspects of Recent Figurative Sculpture.* Cincinnati: The Contemporary Arts Center, 1985.

St. Mary's College Art Gallery. *The Small Format.* Moraga, CA: St. Mary's College, 1973.

———. *The Good Drawing Show.* Moraga, CA: St. Mary's College, 1976.

San Francisco Art Institute. *Other Sources: An American Essay.* San Francisco: San Francisco Art Institute, 1976.

———. *Reflections: Alumni Exhibitions, San Francisco Art Institute.* San Francisco: San Francisco Art Institute, 1982.

San Francisco Museum of Modern Art. *Twenty American Artists.* San Francisco: San Francisco Museum of Modern Art, 1980.

———. *50th Anniversary Commemorative Program 1985.* San Francisco: San Francisco Museum of Modern Art, 1985.

———. *San Francisco Museum of Modern Art: The Painting and Sculpture Collection.* San Francisco: San Francisco Museum of Modern Art, 1985.

San Francisco Museum of Modern Art and the National Collection of Fine Arts, Smithsonian Institution. *Painting and Sculpture in California: The Modern Era.* San Francisco: San Francisco Museum of Modern Art; Washington, DC: National Collection of Fine Arts, Smithsonian Institution, 1976.

Sarah Spurgeon Gallery, Central Washington University. *Second Annual Invitational Drawing Exhibition.* Ellensburg: Sarah Spurgeon Gallery, Central Washington University, 1979.

Schipper, Merle. *Marmo/Marble: A Contemporary Aesthetic.* Los Angeles: California Museum of Science and Industry, 1989.

Scios Nova. *Ventriloquist.* Baltimore: Scios Nova, 1993.

Selz, Peter, ed. *Funk Art.* Berkeley, CA: University Art Museum, 1967.

Southwestern Bell Corporation. *Contemporary Masters Kansas Tour: Selections from the Collection of Southwestern Bell Corporation.* Wichita, KS: Southwestern Bell Corporation, 1988.

Starr, Sandra Leonard. *Lost and Found in California: Four Decades of Assemblage Art.* Santa Monica, CA: James Corcoran Gallery, 1988.

University of Nevada. *1968 Sculpture Invitational.* Reno: University of Nevada, 1968.

Zakian, Michael. *California Figurative Sculpture.* Palm Springs, CA: Palm Springs Desert Museum, 1987.

BROCHURES

American Academy and Institute of Arts and Letters. *36th Annual Purchase Exhibition—Hassam and Speicher Fund.* New York: American Academy and Institute of Arts and Letters, 1984.

Butterfield, Jan. *Manuel Neri: Drawings & Bronzes.* San Francisco: Art Museum Association, 1981.

Charles Cowles Gallery. *Manuel Neri.* New York: Charles Cowles Gallery, 1981.

Community Arts, Inc. *The Downtown Foot Show.* San Francisco: Community Arts, Inc., 1988.

Heyman, Ira Michael, and Elliott, James. *Cal Collects 1.* Berkeley, CA: University Art Museum, 1986.

Leonard, Michael. *The Triumph of the Figure in Bay Area Art: 1950–1965.* San Francisco: 871 Fine Arts, 1987.

The Mexican Museum. *Los Primeros Cinco Años/Fifth Anniversary Exhibit.* San Francisco: The Mexican Museum, 1981.

Museum of Anthropology, California State University. *Sons of the Shaking Earth.* Hayward: California State University, 1983.

Neri, Kate. *Manuel Neri, A Personal Selection.* Belmont, CA: Wiegand Art Gallery, College of Notre Dame, 1988.

Nordland, Gerald. *Manuel Neri.* San Francisco: San Francisco Museum of Art, 1971.

Rodriguez, Peter. *Cinco de Mayo Inaugural Exhibit at the Fort Mason Center.* San Francisco: The Mexican Museum, 1982.

San Francisco Museum of Modern Art. *Resource/Reservoir, CCAC: 75 Years.* San Francisco: San Francisco Museum of Modern Art, 1983.

Sarah Lawrence College Art Gallery. *The United States of the Arts.* Bronxville, NY: Sarah Lawrence College, 1983.

University of California, Davis. *Department of Art.* Davis: University of California Publications, 1982.

Walters, Sylvia Solochek. Introduction to *Counter Visions: Pioneers in Bay Area Art.* San Francisco: Art Department Gallery, San Francisco State University, 1988.

ARTICLES

"Acquisitions." *Artweek,* vol. 16, no. 42, Dec. 14, 1985, p. 9.

Albin, Edgar A. "The Arts: Sculpture Park Offers New Views, Second Chance on Exhibit." *Springfield News-Leader* (Springfield, MO), July 10, 1983.

Albrecht, Herbert. "Die Farbe hat die Plastik Wieder." *Die Welt* (Mannheim, W. Germany), Feb. 18, 1985.

Albright, Thomas. "Rooted in the Tradition of the Human Figure—A Sense of Magical Equilibrium." *San Francisco Chronicle,* Nov. 13, 1971, p. 38.

———. "'Good Drawing Show': Some First-Rate Works at St. Mary's College." *San Francisco Chronicle,* Nov. 1971.

———. "Myth Makers." *Art Gallery,* vol. 18, no. 5, Feb. 1975, pp. 12–17, 44–45.

———. "Neri: Still Sticking with Humans." *San Francisco Chronicle,* Apr. 5, 1975, p. 33.

———. "Manuel Neri: A Kind of Time Warp." *Currant,* vol. 1, no. 1, Apr.–May 1975, pp. 10–16.

———. "Spin-Off." *Artnews,* vol. 74, no. 6, Summer 1975, pp. 113–14.

———. "Santa Cruz: Mecca for Experimental Printmaking." *San Francisco Chronicle,* July 4, 1975.

———. "Top-Notch Studio Offerings." *San Francisco Chronicle,* May 12, 1976, p. 54.

———. "The Magnificence of Manuel Neri." *San Francisco Chronicle,* Sept. 30, 1976, pp. 49–50.

———. "Ron Davis, Then and Now." *Artnews*, vol. 75, no. 9, Nov. 1976, pp. 100–01.

———. "The Cream of the Shows." *San Francisco Chronicle*, Nov. 11, 1976, p. 50.

———. "California Art Since the 'Modern Dawn.'" *Artnews*, Jan. 1977, pp. 68–72.

———. "An Insider's View of Aging." *San Francisco Chronicle*, Sept. 1, 1977, p. 55.

———. "Large Sculpture in Adequate Space." *San Francisco Chronicle*, Nov. 23, 1977, p. 42.

———. "The Possibilities of Hand-Made Paper." *San Francisco Chronicle*, Jan. 13, 1978, p. 44.

———. "Forceful Masterpieces from Manuel Neri." *San Francisco Chronicle*, May 17, 1979, p. 47.

———. "The Growth of Manuel Neri." *San Francisco Chronicle*, Mar. 11, 1980, p. 58.

———. "Bay Area Art: Time of Change." *Horizon*, vol. 23, no. 7, July 1980, pp. 24–35.

———. "A Wide-Ranging Modern Art Exhibition." *S. F. Sunday Examiner & Chronicle*, Aug. 3, 1980, "World" section, pp. 35–36.

———. "Manuel Neri's Survivors: Sculpture for the Age of Anxiety." *Artnews*, vol. 80, no. 1, Jan. 1981, pp. 54–59.

———. "Art Isn't Easily Divided Into Decades." *San Francisco Chronicle*, Feb. 16, 1981.

———. "Neri's Contradictions." *San Francisco Chronicle*, Dec. 3, 1981, p. 76.

———. "San Francisco: Different and Indifferent Drummers." *Artnews*, vol. 81, no. 1, Jan. 1982, pp. 86–90.

———. "Looking Back at a Unique Decade in Art." *San Francisco Chronicle*, Nov. 1, 1982.

———. "Our Public Sculpture—A Disgrace?" *S. F. Sunday Examiner & Chronicle*, Aug. 21, 1983, "Review" section, pp. 11–12.

———. "Magnificent New Figures From Manuel Neri." *San Francisco Chronicle*, Mar. 1, 1984, p. 58.

Ament, Deloris Tarzan. "Engineer Training Shows in Neri's Work." *Seattle Times*, June 8, 1989, pp. F1–2.

"American Academy 1982 Art Awards." *Art World*, Apr. 22, 1982.

Anderson, Wayne. "California Funk and the American Express." *Journal of Art*, vol. 4, no. 6, June/July/Aug. 1991, pp. 65–66.

Applebome, Peter. "The Varied Palette of Hispanic Art in America." *New York Times*, June 21, 1987, "Arts & Leisure" section, p. 31.

"Art Is Thriving in Berkeley—Hayter, Peterdi on Display." *Oakland Tribune*, Dec. 4, 1960, pp. C3, C13.

"Art Magazines: The Pictures are Nice, But . . ." *Oakland Tribune*, June 1, 1975.

"Artists Look at the Crucifixion." *Contra Costa Sun*, Mar. 11, 1992, p. 9.

Artnews, vol. 78, Sept. 1979, p. 118.

"Arts Center Slates Neri Exhibit." *Fresno Bee*, June 28, 1981, p. C5.

Atkins, Richard. "From Photography to Funk." *Horizon*, July/Aug. 1981.

Atkins, Robert D. "A Gallery for Every Salary." *New West*, Mar. 10, 1980, pp. 21–24.

———. "Bay Area Art: Mirror of the Moment." *Scene*, Apr.–May 1982, pp. 9–12.

"Awards of Honor." *Artweek*, vol. 16, no. 23, June 15, 1985, p. 2.

Ayres, Jane. "Important Images in Metal, Stone, Wood." *Times-Tribune* (Palo Alto, CA), Mar. 20, 1988, p. 3.

———. "Braunstein's Art Suppport Stays Strong." *Times-Tribune*, July 4, 1990, "Lifestyle" section.

———. "Three Diverse Artists Showcase New Works in Garden." *Times-Tribune*, Dec. 21, 1990, "Lifestyle" section.

Baker, Kenneth. "Legacy of a Journalist/Historian." *S. F. Sunday Examiner & Chronicle*, June 23, 1985, "Review" section, pp. 1, 12–13.

———. "A Modest and Upbeat Show of Sculpture." *S. F. Sunday Examiner & Chronicle*, July 27, 1986, "Review" section, pp. 12–13.

———. "Crown Press Moves to SOMA; New Berggruen Space." *San Francisco Chronicle*, Oct. 16, 1986, p. 60.

———. "Home-Grown Sculpture." *San Francisco Chronicle*, Mar. 31, 1988, p. E2.

———. "The Two Sides of Manuel Neri." *San Francisco Chronicle*, May 17, 1988, p. E2.

———. "Powerhouse of Figurative Painting." *San Francisco Chronicle*, May 28, 1989.

———. "Odd Poses Lend Tension to Manuel Neri's Sculptures." *San Francisco Chronicle*, June 4, 1989, "Review" section, pp. 14–15.

———. "Viola Frey's Ceramic Mysteries." *San Francisco Chronicle*, Mar. 31, 1990, p. C5.

———. "Sublimated Eroticism and Frenzied Funk." *San Francisco Chronicle*, Sept. 10, 1993, pp. 42–43.

"Un Ballo in Maschera." *San Francisco Opera Magazine*, 1977.

Bloomfield, Arthur. "Sculptor's Boxing Packs No Punch." *San Francisco Examiner*, Aug. 12, 1966.

———. "20 Years of San Francisco Sculpture." *San Francisco Examiner*, Feb. 5, 1976, p. 24.

———. "Out of the Piazzas With Extra Pizzazz." *San Francisco Examiner*, Nov. 22, 1977.

Blum, Walter. "A Showcase for Contemporary Art." *San Francisco Examiner*, Aug. 10, 1980, pp. 16–20.

Boettger, Suzaan. "Manuel Neri—Recent Work." *Artweek*, Sept. 13, 1977, p. 7.

"Book Explores Artist's Relationship with 20-year Model." *Neighbor Want Ads* (Atlanta), Apr. 1991, p. 7A.

Braff, Phyllis. "Manuel Neri's Life-Size Figures at the Dia." *New York Times*, Aug. 29, 1993, p. 16.

Brenson, Michael. "Figurative Sculpture of the 80's." *New York Times*, June 13, 1986, p. C1.

———. "Plaster as a Medium, Not Just an Interim Step." *New York Times*, June 1990.

———. "The State of the City as Sculptors See It." *New York Times*, July 27, 1990, pp. C1, C22.

Brzezinski, Jamey. "A Printmaker's Paradise." *Artweek*, Nov. 21, 1991, p. 9.

"Bronze Show Continues." *Encore!* (Reno, NV), July 1986, p. 3.

Brooks, Valerie F. "The State of Contemporary Sculpture." *MD*, Feb. 1983, pp. 59–66.

Brown, Erica. "Precision with Playfulness." *New York Times*, July 9, 1979, Sunday magazine, p. 53.

Brumfield, John. "The Olympics California Sculpture Show." *Artweek*, vol. 15, no. 27, July 28, 1984, p. 1.

Burkhart, Dorothy. "Splashy Figures at Mexican Museum: Manuel Neri's Sculptures Show Mysterious Quality." *San Jose Mercury News*, June 7, 1981, "The Tab," pp. 10–11.

———. "Battered Forms Put Humanity Back on Display." *San Jose Mercury News*, Sept. 23, 1982, pp. 1D, 7D.

———. "The 60's Art Experience." *San Jose Mercury News*, Oct. 17, 1982, "The Tab," pp. 1A–8A.

———. "The Figure's Beauty Realized in the Abstract." *San Jose Mercury News*, June 4, 1989.

Butterfield, Jan. "Ancient Auras—Expressionist Angst: Sculpture by Manuel Neri." *Images and Issues*, Spring 1981, pp. 38–43.

Caen, Herb. "Along the Presidio." *Architectural Digest*, Dec. 1985, pp. 118–26.

Caldwell, Sandra. "Manuel Neri, Sculptor." *Oakland Museum Bulletin*, Sept. 1976.

Carlsen, Peter. "Elements of Style." *Architectural Digest*, Nov. 1985, pp. 150–56.

Casasco, Ermanno. "La Casa di Una Collezionista d'Arte Moderna: Paule Anglim." *Casa & Giardino* (Milano, Italy), no. 132, May 1983, pp. 40–45.

Cathro, Morton. "Taking up the Cross." *Oakland Tribune*, Mar. 29, 1992, p. 2C.

Chipp, Herschel B. "Exhibition in San Francisco." *Artnews*, vol. 59, no. 6, Oct. 1960, p. 50.

Ciaffardini, David. "What's A Noted Artist Doing in a Place Like This?" *Vacaville Reporter*, Jan. 31, 1982, pp. 1A, 8A.

"Circle of Styles on the West Coast." *Art in America*, vol. 52, no. 3, June 1964, p. 30.

Cohn, Terri. "Abstraction and Figuration Integrated." *Artweek*, vol. 20, no. 25, July 15, 1989, p. 3.

Coke, Van Deren. "Bay Area Art of the 50s and 60s, the Gift of Dr. Samuel West." *Bulletin, The University of New Mexico Art Museum*, no. 11, 1977–78, pp. 6–13.

Collins, Meghan. "Benicia's Lively Arts." *Art Well*, Mar./Apr. 1984, pp. 4–5.

Cope, Penelope Bass. "Public Sculptures Polish the Gateway." *Sunday News Journal* (Wilmington, DE), Aug. 21, 1988, pp. K1, K3.

Coplans, John. "Sculpture in California." *Artforum*, Aug. 1963, pp. 3–6.

———. "The Nude: Drawings by Alvin Light, Manuel Neri, Gordon Cook, Joan Brown." *Artforum*, Nov. 1963, p. 39.

———. "Abstract Expressionist Ceramics." *Artforum*, vol. 5, no. 3, Nov. 1966, pp. 34–41.

Coplans, John, and Leider, Philip. "West Coast Art: Three Images." *Artforum*, vol. 1, no. 12, June 1963, pp. 21–25.

Cotter, Colleen. "Major Exhibit of Bronzes on Display at Museum." *Record Searchlight* (Redding, CA), May 1985.

"The Crucifixion." *San Mateo Times*, Mar. 11, 1992, p. 20.

Dalkey, Victoria. "Icons of the Flesh." *Sacramento Bee,* Nov. 3, 1985, "Encore" section, p. 28.

———. "Cultural Crossroads." *Horizon,* vol. 31, no. 1, Jan./Feb. 1988, "Valley Arts" section, pp. 12–14.

———. "Forms of Expression." *Sacramento Bee,* Aug. 26, 1990, "Encore" section, p. 10.

Delatiner, Barbara. "Nassau Museum Ready to be Open." *New York Times,* June 1, 1980.

Delehanty, Hugh J. "Manuel Neri: Cast From A Different Mold." *Focus Magazine,* Jan. 1982, pp. 24–27.

Delmar, John Davies. "A Cast of Artists Who Shape in Plaster." *Newsday,* June 19, 1990, part 2, p. 11.

Donnelly, Kathleen. "How Much House Does $2 Million Buy?" *Palo Alto Weekly* (Palo Alto, CA), Oct. 9, 1985, p. 3A.

Donohue, Marlena. "The Galleries." *Los Angeles Times,* Nov. 4, 1988, part 6, p. 15.

Drohojowska, Hunter. "A Northwestern Passage." *Architectural Digest,* Sept. 1990, pp. 196–201.

Dunham, Judith. "Images of Woman." *Artweek,* vol. 6, no. 41, Nov. 29, 1975, pp. 13–14.

———. "Manuel Neri: Life with the Figure." *Artweek,* Nov. 13, 1976, pp. 1, 7.

———. "Stars, Stripes and Celebrities." *Artweek,* Aug. 30, 1980, pp. 1, 9.

Evans, Ingrid. "Notes from a Nevada History." *Artweek,* vol. 18, no. 19, May 16, 1987, p. 1.

———. "Funk and Figurative." *Reno Gazette-Journal,* Mar. 12, 1989.

"Events." *Sculpture,* May/June 1987, p. 41.

Feeser, Sigrid. "Frischer Wind von der Westkuste." *Rheinpfalz* (Mannheim, W. Germany), Feb. 8, 1985.

"Fighting Apartheid at Michael Jackson's." *San Francisco Chronicle,* Apr. 8, 1988, p. 5B.

Figoten, Sheldon. "Building and Painting the Figure." *Artweek,* June 20, 1981, pp. 5–6.

"Foster/White Gallery: National Sculpture Exhibition, 1987." *Signature* (Edmonds, WA), Feb. 1987, p. 6.

"Four Drawings: Manuel Neri." *Artforum,* vol. 2, no. 10, Apr. 1964, pp. 32–33.

Fowler, Carol. "Artists of Modern Times Consider the Crucifixion." *Contra Costa Times* (Contra Costa, CA), Mar. 28, 1992, p. 2C.

Frank, Peter. "Manuel Neri (Braunstein/Quay)." *Artnews,* vol. 75, no. 5, May 1976, p. 128.

Frankenstein, Alfred. "In '71—A Controversial Fountain, A Merger and Acquisitions." *S. F. Sunday Examiner & Chronicle,* Jan. 2, 1972, "This World" section, pp. 37–38.

———. "The Old and the New in Oakland Shows." *S. F. Sunday Examiner & Chronicle,* May 28, 1972, "This World" section, pp. 34–35.

———. "Hansen Fuller Commemorative." *San Francisco Chronicle,* Oct. 30, 1975.

———. "A Gallery Full of Sculpture." *San Francisco Chronicle,* Jan. 29, 1976, p. 36.

———. "Public Art and The Abstracts in The Modern Era." *S. F. Sunday Examiner & Chronicle,* Sept. 19, 1976, "This World" section, p. 35.

———. "Innovative Sculptor of the Life Cast." *San Francisco Chronicle,* Feb. 25, 1979, p. 49.

Frantzis, Peggy. "Triton Adds 3 Works to Sculpture Garden." *Santa Clara Valley Weekly,* Jan. 3, 1991, p. 2.

French, Christopher. "Portraits of Artists." *Artweek,* Oct. 30, 1982, p. 11.

———. "Manuel Neri: Figures Out of Time." *Artweek,* vol. 15, no. 11, Mar. 17, 1984, p. 1.

———. "Looking Back to the Dilexi." *Artweek,* vol. 15, no. 37, Nov. 3, 1984, p. 1.

———. "Art in the San Francisco Bay Area." *The Museum of California* (The Oakland Museum), July/Aug. 1985, pp. 13–16.

Fribourgh, Cindy. "Photographs, Bronzes Shown at Arts Center." *Arkansas Democrat,* Apr. 4, 1982.

Fried, Alexander. "Violent Fantasy in Art." *San Francisco Chronicle,* Feb. 1959.

Friedlander, Lisa M. "Pair Collaborate on Limited Edition." *Arts Benicia,* July/Aug. 1992, pp. 1, 5, 7.

"From Humans to Boxes." *San Francisco Chronicle,* Aug. 1966.

Fuller, Mary. "San Francisco Sculpture." *Art in America,* vol. 52, June 1964, pp. 52–59.

Gale, Andrew. "Art Views: Limited Ceramics, Sculpture Which Searches to Believe." *Sacramento Bee,* Mar. 26, 1972, "Leisure" section, pp. 10–11.

Garcia, John. "Once They Sneered, Now Artists Get Plastered." *Daily News* (New York), June 8, 1990.

Garver, Thomas. "Omaha: Space-Rich and Hungry for Art." *Artnews,* vol. 87, no. 5, May 1988, pp. 31–32.

Gerard, Paul. "Paper Route." *Isthmus* (Madison, WI), Dec. 4, 1987, p. 32.

Gidfrey, Dominique. "Art Contemporain à Bordeaux: Un Octobre Californien." *TV Loisirs* (Bordeaux, France), Sept. 16, 1984, p. 35.

Gimelson, Deborah. "Los Angeles Redux." *Art & Auction,* Mar. 1988, p. 54.

Glowen, Ron. "Neri's Figures Are Striking and Gaunt—ART SHOW." *Everett Herald,* Feb. 5, 1981, p. 2C.

Goldberger, Paul. "Architecture: Robert A. M. Stern." *Architectural Digest,* October 1990, pp. 196–205.

Gomez, Edward M. "The San Francisco Rebellion." *Time,* Feb. 5, 1990, pp. 74–75.

Gordon, Harvey. "'Sculptors on Paper' Disappoints, Lacks Substance." *Kalamazoo Gazette,* Sept. 16, 1988.

Gottlieb, Shirley. "The Human Body: Back But Never Gone." *Long Beach Press Telegram,* Apr. 4, 1984.

Graham, Barbara. "Art Attack at 80 Langton." *Focus Magazine,* Dec. 1981, pp. 22–25.

Green, Blake. "Yuppies Discover Art." *San Francisco Chronicle,* Sept. 1, 1987, pp. 15, 17.

Hackett, Regina. "Woman's Many Facets." *Artweek,* vol. 6, no. 41, Nov. 29, 1975, pp. 13–14.

———. "SAM Exhibit Pushes Beyond Stereotypes." *Seattle Post-Intelligencer,* Feb. 1, 1981, pp. H7–8.

———. "30 Years of American Sculpture." *Seattle Post-Intelligencer,* Nov. 15, 1984, pp. C1, C9.

———. "Neri Work is a First for Seattle." *Seattle Post-Intelligencer,* Sept. 4, 1991, p. C6.

Hagan, R. H. "Dilexi: To Select, to Value, to Love." *The Museum of California* (The Oakland Museum), Sept./Oct. 1984, pp. 11–13.

Hale, David. "Bronze Making a Big Comeback in FSU Exhibit." *Fresno Bee,* Sept. 22, 1986, p. G12.

Hamlin, Jesse. "Art Auction at Michael Jackson's House." *San Francisco Chronicle,* Apr. 11, 1988, p. 2A.

Hancock, Lorie. "Real Art is Really Good." *Union* (Long Beach, CA), Mar. 22, 1984, p. 6.

Harper, Paula. "Sculptor's Nudes Embody Mankind." *Miami News,* Nov. 5, 1982.

Hartness, Ruth. "Top Choices Strong but Restrained." *Creative Loafing* (Atlanta), July 30, 1988, p. 4B.

Hazard, Paul. "The Northwest: This Month's Tour From Michigan to California." *Horizon,* Jan. 1981, pp. 25–29.

Heartney, Eleanor. "Manuel Neri at Charles Cowles." *Art in America,* vol. 79, no. 5, May 1991, pp. 175–76.

Hemphill, Chris. "Sculptural Drama." *Architectural Digest,* Mar. 1980, pp. 68, 120.

Hendricks, Mark. "Bay Area Exhibit Paints Diverse Styles, Movements." *Daily Nebraskan,* Oct. 4, 1984, pp. 11–12.

Hoffman, Donald. "Figures Show Masterful Ways of Working with Bronze." *Kansas City Star,* Feb. 23, 1986, p. 9D.

Huber, Alfred. "Wenn die Linie einen Bogen kreuzt." *Mannheimer Morgen* (Mannheim, W. Germany), Feb. 4, 1985.

Hughes, Robert. "Heritage of Rich Imagery." *Time,* vol. 132, no. 2, July 11, 1988, pp. 62–64.

Hurlburt, Roger. "A Celebration of Life and Limb." *News/Sun Sentinel,* Feb. 7, 1988, p. 3F.

ICA News (University of California, San Diego), vol. 1, no. 3, Spring 1984.

"In The Galleries." *ArtTalk,* Mar. 1992, p. 42.

Jinkner-Lloyd, Amy. "'Top Choices' Few in Number, Strong in Content." *Atlanta Journal,* July 27, 1988, p. 3C.

Johnsrud, Even Hebbe. "Fantasi-utfordring." *Aftenposten* (Oslo, Norway), Sept. 13, 1985.

Jones, Marianna. "Manuel Neri: Obsession with Depicting Human Forms Distinguishes Californian's Art Work." *Walla Walla Union Bulletin,* Apr. 3, 1980.

Juris, Prudence. "Neri's Second Skins." *Artweek,* vol. 2, no. 41, Nov. 27, 1971, p. 12.

———. "Interview with Sam West: Collecting 'Of Our Time and Our Community.'" *San Francisco Progress,* July 28, 1972.

Kangas, Matthew. "Rebirth of Venus." *Sculpture,* vol. 9, no. 6, Nov./Dec. 1990, pp. 48–55.

Kattman, Sarah. "Living Theater." *House Beautiful,* Nov. 1991, pp. 75–83.

Kaufman, Charles. "Neri Leads New Exhibits at Arts Center." *Arkansas Gazette* (Little Rock), Apr. 2, 1982, p. 1C.

Kimmelman, Michael. "30 Hispanic Artists at the Brooklyn Museum." *New York Times,* June 9, 1989, p. B12.

Klein, Elaine. "New Exhibit Offers Look into Sculptors' Thoughts." *Kalamazoo Gazette,* Sept. 11, 1988, p. H1.

Kohen, Helen L. "Sculpting the Everyman in Brash, Bold Bronze." *Miami Herald,* Oct. 29, 1982, p. 2D.

———. "Art Looks for a Place in the Sun." *Artnews,* vol. 82, no. 2, Feb. 1983, pp. 62–65.

"Kooky Group Repair Show." *San Francisco Chronicle,* Mar. 1969.

Kramer, Hilton. "Art: First Solo Show for Manuel Neri." *New York Times,* Feb. 27, 1981.

"La Maison Blanche." *Maison & Jardin* (France), Mar. 1991.

Lee, Anthony. "The Gang of Six." *Artweek,* vol. 21, no. 3, Jan. 25, 1990, pp. 1, 20.

Leider, Philip. "Manuel Neri." *Artforum,* Sept. 1963, p. 45.

———. "California After the Figure." *Art in America,* vol. 51, no. 5, Oct. 1963, p. 77.

Le Van, Brook B. "The Bemis Experience." *Sculpture,* vol. 7, no. 3, May/June 1988, pp. 26–27.

Lewis, Jo Ann. "Peopled Paradox." *Washington Post,* Feb. 3, 1983.

Lofstrom, Mark. "Character of Our Age & History in Sculpture." *Cultural Climate* (Honolulu), Apr. 1983, p. 7.

Long, Robert. "Artist's Style Presents Paradox." *Southampton Press,* Sept. 9, 1993, pp. 21, 24.

Macias, Sandra. "Getting a Handle on Sculpture." *Reno Gazette-Journal,* June 29, 1986, p. 5E.

MacMillan, Kyle. "Sculptors Confront Limitations of Two Dimensions." *Sunday World Herald* (Lincoln, NE), Apr. 9, 1989, "Entertainment" section.

Magloff, Joanna. "California Sculpture at the Oakland Museum." *Artnews,* vol. 62, no. 9, Jan. 1964, p. 51.

"Manuel Neri." *Art Well,* Mar./Apr. 1984, p. 23.

"Manuel Neri at Middendorf/Lane." *Art Now/U.S.A.: The National Art Museum and Gallery Guide,* Feb./Mar. 1983, p. NY9.

"Manuel Neri: Escultura y Dibujos." *Art Nexus,* May 1991, pp. 112–13.

"Manuel Neri Exhibit at Park." *St. Louis Post-Dispatch,* June 23, 1983.

"Manuel Neri: Woman." *Artweek,* vol. 6, no. 16, Apr. 19, 1975.

Marger, Mary Ann. "Sculpture Unveiled at Bank Building." *St. Petersburg Times* (Florida), Mar. 31, 1988, "Tampa" section, p. 3.

Marlowe, John. "Power, Politics and Publicity, but Is It Art?" *San Francisco Magazine,* vol. 2, no. 5, May 1988, pp. 20–24, 123.

Marmer, Nancy. "Los Angeles." *Artforum,* vol. 3, no. 4, Jan. 1965, pp. 13–14.

McCann, Cecile N. "Geis and Neri at SFAI." *Artweek,* vol. 1, no. 31, Sept. 26, 1970, p. 3.

McColm, Del. "Blockbuster Show of Recent UCD Art Exhibited." *Davis Enterprise* (Davis, CA), Oct. 17, 1980.

———. "Sculptures Dominate." *Davis Enterprise,* Mar. 22, 1984.

———. "Fantasies Fulfilled." *Davis Enterprise,* Apr. 5, 1984.

McDevitt, Lorelei Heller. "Inspired by a Collection." *Designers West,* vol. 34, no. 6, Apr. 1987, pp. 84–88, 168.

McDonald, Robert. "Manuel Neri." *Artweek,* June 2, 1979, pp. 1, 19.

McKinley, Cameron Curtis. "Adaptability: A Personal Expression in a Designer's Own San Francisco Home." *Architectural Digest,* Nov. 1982, pp. 104–11.

McRae, Jacqueline. "Visions in Bronze." *Walla-Walla Union Bulletin,* Nov. 17, 1988.

Medina, Danny. "Manuel Neri." *Art Talk,* Feb. 1991, pp. 28–29.

———. "Danny's Column." *Art Talk,* Sept. 1992, p. 41.

Meisel, Alan. "Letter from San Francisco." *Craft Horizons,* vol. 31, Dec. 1971, p. 55.

Mennin, Mark. "Innovations with the Figure: The Sculpture of Manuel Neri." *Arts,* vol. 60, no. 8, Apr. 1986, pp. 76–77.

Merritt, Robert. "'Sculpture Now' Unsettling." *Richmond Times-Dispatch,* Oct. 14, 1983.

Michael, Peggy. "Sculptors on Paper." *FORUM* (Kalamazoo Institute of the Arts), vol. 1, no. 2, Sept. 1988.

Mills, Paul. "Bay Area Figurative." *Art in America,* vol. 52, no. 3, June 1964, p. 44.

Monte, James. "Manuel Neri and Wayne Thiebaud." *Artforum,* vol. 3, no. 44, Mar. 1965.

Morch, Al. "San Francisco." *Artforum,* vol. 5, no. 2, Oct. 1966, p. 56.

———. "We're Still in the Bronze Age." *San Francisco Examiner,* Aug. 2, 1982, p. E6.

———. "S/12: Sculpture around the Bay." *San Francisco Examiner,* Aug. 4, 1982, p. E6.

Morris, Gay. "Sculptor Manuel Neri brings Figurative Influence to the Female Form." *Oakland Tribune,* May 30, 1989.

———. "Report from San Francisco: Figures by the Bay." *Art in America,* vol. 78, no. 11, Nov. 1990, pp. 90–97.

Morse, Marcia. "A Fascination for the Human Figure." *Sunday Star-Bulletin and Advertiser* (Honolulu), May 8, 1983.

Moss, Stacey. "Neri Sculptures: An Art Show that Renews the Faith." *Peninsula Times Tribune* (Palo Alto, CA), May 25, 1979, pp. C1, C11.

———. "The Oakland Museum Struts its Stuff in Style." *Peninsula Times Tribune,* Nov. 5, 1979, p. C4.

Nadaner, Dan. "Direct Marks and Layers of Mystery." *Artweek,* vol. 18, no. 21, May 30, 1987, p. 1.

"National Sculpture Show at Foster/White Gallery." *Seattle Guide,* Feb. 1987, p. 8.

Neri, Manuel. "Chan-Chan." *Artweek,* vol. 6, no. 14, Apr. 5, 1965.

"Neri Plasters Critic." *University of California at Davis Aggie,* Nov. 1, 1972.

"Neri Posture." *S. F. Sunday Examiner & Chronicle,* June 7, 1981.

"Neri's Quartet." *San Francisco Chronicle,* Sept. 30, 1976, p. 50.

"Neri Takes on Local Figurative Movement with Sculptures." *Alameda Times Star* (Alameda, CA), June 2, 1989.

"Neri Works Featured in Laumeier Exhibition." *St. Louis Weekly,* June 29, 1983, p. 33.

Neumann-Cosel-Nebe, Isabelle von. "Olympischer Nachgeschmack." *Rhein-Neckar-Zeitung* (Mannheim, W. Germany), Mar. 5, 1985.

"New Contemporary Gallery." *Artweek,* vol. 1, no. 2, Jan. 10, 1970, p. 2.

"New Gallery Lures Back Some Artists." *San Francisco Chronicle,* Dec. 18, 1969.

Nieto, Margarita. "Manuel Neri." *Latin American Art,* vol. 1, no. 2, Fall 1989, pp. 52–56.

Nixon, Bruce. "The Way Things Were." *Artweek,* vol. 21, no. 1, Jan. 11, 1990, pp. 1, 8.

"Northern California's Guggenheims." *San Francisco Chronicle,* Apr. 12, 1979, p. 27.

Northington, Suzanne. "John Berggruen: High Priest of Price-Tag Art." *San Francisco Magazine,* vol. 1, no. 2, Feb. 1987, pp. 32–36, 70.

Northwood, Bill. "S12: Sculptural Bonanza." *The Museum of California* (The Oakland Museum), July/Aug. 1982, pp. 4–5.

"On the Road." *Artweek,* vol. 15, no. 18, May 5, 1984, p. 10.

O'Neil, Mollie. "All About Birds." *Artweek,* Oct. 14, 1972.

"Pacific Art Festival Award." *Oakland Tribune,* Oct. 1, 1952, p. 20.

"Un 'passaporto' da scultore." *Nazione Carrara* (Carrara, Italy), Nov. 20, 1987.

Paulsen, Jane. "Living with Her Livelihood." *SF,* Aug. 1990, pp. 80–85.

"Pedro Rodriguez: Fundador del Museo de Arte Mexicano en San Francisco y Representante del Chicano en Ambos Paises." *El Sol de Mexico en la Cultura,* Feb. 28, 1982, pp. 4–5.

Perkins, Janet. "A Glimpse into Other Worlds." *UC Davis Magazine,* Summer 1992, pp. 22–23.

Pincus, Robert L. "The Making of Manuel Neri." *Sculpture,* Jan./Feb. 1994, pp. 34–37.

Polley, E. M. "Benicia Area is Now Seen as Newest Haven for Varied Artists, Craftsmen." *Sunday Times-Herald* (Benicia, CA), Aug. 14, 1966, p. W8.

"The Prospect Over the Bay." *Arts,* vol. 37, no. 4, May–June 1963, p. 20.

Reuter, Laurel. "Bronze Casting." *Grand Forks Herald* (Grand Forks, ND), Oct. 3, 1986, p. 8D.

"Review." *Artforum,* vol. 1, no. 5, Oct. 1962, p. 39.

Rice, Nancy N. "Manuel Neri." *New Art Examiner,* Oct. 1983, p. 21.

Richardson, Brenda. "Bay Area Survey." *Arts,* vol. 45, no. 1, Sept. 1970, pp. 52–53.

Robins, Cynthia. "AIDS Art Benefit to Open May 18." *San Francisco Chronicle,* Mar. 30, 1989, p. A10.

Robinson, Teri. "The Art of Giving." *UC Davis Magazine,* vol. 2, no. 3, Winter 1985, pp. 16–19.

Roder, Sylvie. "A Look at Collections." *Artweek,* vol. 16, no. 14, Apr. 6, 1985, p. 3.

———. "A Sampling of Sculpture." *Palo Alto Weekly* (Palo Alto, CA), Mar. 2, 1988, p. 32.

Ronck, Ronn. "Manuel Neri." *Honolulu Advertiser,* May 3, 1983.

Rubin, Michael G. "Neri Sculpture at Laumeier." *St. Louis Globe-Democrat,* July 2–3, 1983, p. 7E.

"San Francisco." *Artforum,* vol. 9, no. 3, Nov. 1970, pp. 89–90.

"San Francisco." *Arts,* vol. 39, no. 1, Oct. 1964, pp. 23, 25.

"San Francisco Art Institute Exhibition." *Arts,* vol. 45, no. 1, Sept. 1970, pp. 52–53.

"San Francisco: Manuel Neri at Paule Anglim." *Art in America,* Oct. 1979.

"San Francisco Museum of Modern Art." *San Francisco Focus,* June 1989, pp. 128, 135.

"San Francisco Sculptor Neri Given Art Award." *San Francisco Chronicle,* May 9, 1959.

Sanders, Luanne. "Manuel and Mary." *Creative Loafing,* Apr. 20, 1991, pp. 69–70.

Scarborough, James. "A Dialog of Color and Form." *Artweek,* vol. 18, no. 16, Apr. 25, 1987, p. 4.

Scarborough, Jessica. "Sculptural Paper: Foundations and Directions." *Fiberarts,* vol. 2, no. 2, Mar./Apr. 1984, pp. 32–35, 73.

Schlesinger, Norma. *Sausalito Review,* no. 40, Feb. 1979, p. 21.

———. "The Art Review." *Sausalito Review,* Jan./Feb. 1981, p. 15.

———. "A Modern Medici." *Sausalito Review,* Oct. 1982, p. 15.

Schwartz, Joyce Pomeroy. "Public Art." *Encyclopedia of Architecture (Design, Engineering & Construction),* vol. 4, 1990, pp. 112–39.

"Sculpting a Niche in Modern Art." *Marin Independent Journal* (San Rafael, CA), June 5, 1989, p. D5.

"Sculptor Manuel Neri to Lead Art Lecture Series." *Baton Rouge Advocate,* Feb. 6, 1983.

"Sculpture Exhibits Open in Santa Rosa." *Argus-Courier* (Santa Rosa, CA), Nov. 4, 1977, p. 6B.

"Sculpture 1982/ISC12 and Beyond." *Images & Issues,* Nov./Dec. 1982, pp. 38–50.

Seehafer, Mary. "Injecting Bold Style into a City Co-op." *House & Garden,* Mar. 1982, pp. 118–20.

Selz, Peter. "A Modern Looks at Itself: San Francisco." *Arts,* vol. 59, no. 8, Apr. 1985, pp. 87–93.

———. "Art in the San Francisco Bay Area, 1945–1980." *California Monthly,* vol. 96, no. 2, Dec. 1985, p. 10.

Seymour, Ann. "Gallery Owners and Artists: Adversaries or Partners?" *Nob Hill Gazette* (San Francisco, CA), May 1984, pp. 21, 23.

———. "The Vision of San Francisco." *San Francisco Magazine,* vol. 2, no. 5, May 1988, pp. 32–37, 124.

Shere, Charles. "The Figurative Tradition Gets Triple Boost." *Oakland Tribune,* Apr. 20, 1975.

———. "Impressive Showing of Bay Sculpture." *Oakland Tribune,* Feb. 22, 1976, p. E18.

———. "Show by Sculptor-Painter Neri One of Magnificence." *Oakland Tribune,* Dec. 3, 1981, pp. D14–15.

———. "Sculpture that is Drawing with Vitality." *Oakland Tribune,* Jan. 21, 1982, p. I24.

———. "A Resort and a Park Become Galleries." *Oakland Tribune,* Sept. 26, 1982, pp. H3–H5.

———. "An Exhibit Looks at the '60s." *Oakland Tribune,* Nov. 7, 1982, p. H25.

———. "A Long-Awaited Ode to California Art." *Oakland Tribune,* May 24, 1985.

———. "Oakland Museum Show Strains to Cover Rich Bay Area Art Scene since 1945." *Oakland Tribune,* June 21, 1985, p. D3.

Slivka, Rose C. S. "From the Studio." *East Hampton Star,* Aug. 12, 1993, p. II9.

"Slouching Mortality and Inky Galaxies." *Artnews,* Jan. 1977.

Smallwood, Lyn. "Manuel Neri Lets the Ghosts of Art History Surface from His Sculptures." *Seattle Post-Intelligencer,* June 8, 1989, p. C7.

Snoeyenbos, Theresa. "Works by Expressionist Artist Displayed." *NewsPress Weekender* (OK), Oct. 9, 1981, pp. 1–2.

Somlo, Patty. "A Place in Time: Bay Area Figurative Art." *San Francisco Chronicle,* Sept. 16, 1990, "Review" section, p. 4.

Speer, Robert. "Manuel Neri's 'Spirit Figures.'" *Chico News & Review* (Chico, CA) Mar. 29, 1984, p. 45.

Stack, Peter. "Airport Shoes: One Show Fits All." *San Francisco Chronicle,* Dec. 2, 1987, p. E1.

Stamets, Russell A. "Art Center Exhibits Bat One-for-Three." *Wisconsin State Journal* (Madison, WI), Dec. 17, 1987, section 4.

"Statue Study." *Sacramento Bee,* Apr. 2, 1982.

Steele, Nancy. "Neri Retrospective." *Benicia Herald,* May 28, 1989, p. 6.

Steele, Sabrina. "Art Exhibit Explores Human Form." *Daily Forty-Niner* (California State University, Long Beach), Apr. 12, 1984, p. 5.

Stein, Ruthe. "A Makeshift Movement." *San Francisco Chronicle,* Dec. 13, 1989, pp. B3, B5.

Stiles, Knute. "San Francisco." *Artforum,* vol. 10, no. 3, Nov. 1971, pp. 87–88.

———. "Manuel Neri at the Oakland Museum and Braunstein Quay." *Art in America,* Jan. 1977, p. 131.

———. "San Francisco: Manuel Neri at Paule Anglim." *Art in America,* Oct. 1979.

Stofflet, Mary. "Twenty American Artists at S.F. Museum of Modern Art." *Images & Issues,* vol. 1, no. 3, Winter 1980–81, p. 44.

Szabat, A. M. "'Sculptures on Paper' Serves as Letters of Introduction to Most Lincolnites." *Lincoln Journal* (Lincoln, NE), Mar. 19, 1989.

Tarshis, Jerome. "Art in Northern California Since 1960: Anything Goes." *Portfolio,* July/Aug. 1983, pp. 44–51.

———. "Jazz Shapes Caught in Marble." *Christian Science Monitor,* Oct. 4, 1988, pp. 30–31.

Tarzan, Deloris. "Pair of Contemporary Painters Offer Exhibit of Freewheeling Arts." *Seattle Times,* Jan. 22, 1981.

Taylor, Dan. "Bronze Look." *Press Democrat* (Sonoma, CA), Oct. 19, 1984.

Taylor, Joan Chatfield. "In San Francisco." *Architectural Digest,* vol. 48, no. 2, Feb. 1991, pp. 116–23.

Temko, Allan. "Olé! It's Already a Triumph." *San Francisco Chronicle,* Dec. 28, 1980, pp. 13–14.

———. "The Odd Couple of Ethnic Art." *San Francisco Chronicle,* June 18, 1981.

"The Third World Painting and Sculpture." *Artweek,* vol. 15, no. 24, July 13, 1974, p. 4.

The Threepenny Review, vol. 5, no. 1, Spring 1984.

Tromble, Meredith. "A Conversation with Manuel Neri." *Artweek,* Apr. 8, 1993, p. 20.

Tuchman, Phyllis. "A Sculptor Captive to Body Language of the Female Form." *Newsday,* Feb. 16, 1986, part 2, p. 15.

———. "The Sunshine Boys." *Connoisseur,* vol. 217, no. 901, Feb. 1987, pp. 62–69.

"Two Views of the Figure: Neri, Adair, Art in Berkeley." *Oakland Tribune,* May 10, 1964, p. 5.

Van Proyen, Mark. "Commemorating a Critic's Eye." *Artweek,* vol. 16, no. 25, July 13, 1985, p. 1.

———. "Nuances of the Particular." *Artweek,* vol. 18, no. 37, Nov. 7, 1987, p. 1.

Venturi, Anita. "San Francisco: A Field Day for Sculptors." *Arts,* vol. 38, no. 1, Oct. 1963, p. 64.

———. "Manuel Neri." *Contemporary Sculpture: Arts Yearbook 8,* 1965, p. 138.

———. "The Prospect over the Bay." *Arts,* May 1963, pp. 19–21.

Villani, John. "Small Presses Have A Lot to Say about Quality Says Owner of One." *Pasatiempo,* Dec. 6, 1991, pp. 13, 42.

"Visual Arts." *Walla-Walla Union Bulletin,* Nov. 10, 1988, p. 14.

"Walking the Night Away: Second Summer Gallery Openings Friday." *Journal Newspapers* (Ketchum, ID), July 3, 1991, pp. 6B, 12B.

Wallace, Dean. "Action Sculpture by Manuel Neri." *San Francisco Chronicle,* July 1980.

Watson, Lloyd. "'Mr. Carneros' Switching from Wine to Art." *San Francisco Chronicle,* Feb. 5, 1986, p. 25.

———. "French Unveil $35 Million S.F. Realty 'Toe-Hold.'" *San Francisco Chronicle,* Mar. 1, 1989, p. C3.

Webster, Mary Hull. "Mysteries of Death and Light." *Artweek,* Apr. 23, 1992, p. 20.

Weddington, Diane. "College to Show Provocative Artwork on Jesus' Crucifixion." *Contra Costa Times,* Mar. 7, 1992, p. 4D.

"Weekend's Best." *Press Democrat* (Santa Rosa, CA), Dec. 7, 1984, p. 3E.

Weeks, H. J. "Bay Area Sculpture Survey." *Artweek,* vol. 7, no. 10, Mar. 6, 1976, p. 9.

Weisang, Miriam. "The Mexican Museum." *Northern California Home and Garden,* vol. 2, no. 7, May 1989, pp. 38–44, 87.

Weisburg, Ruth. "Ten Sculptors Working with the Figure." *Artweek,* vol. 15, no. 15, Apr. 14, 1984, p. 1.

Wells, Peggy Sue. "Engineering to Sculpturing." *Benicia Herald,* July 9, 1980, p. 10.

Where—San Francisco, June 5–8, 1989.

Wiley-Robertson, Salli. "Art in the Bay Area: 1945–1980." *Art & Antique Collector,* vol. 2, no. 10, Aug. 1985, pp. 14–16.

Wilson, William. "Sculpture: California Dreaming." *Los Angeles Times,* Aug. 29, 1982, "Calendar" section, p. 82.

Winokur, Scott. "Manuel Neri—At Home with His Plaster Ladies." *Oakland Tribune,* Mar. 2, 1977, pp. 15–18.

Winter, David. "Reliving Northern California Art of the Sixties." *Peninsula Times Tribune* (Palo Alto, CA), Nov. 2, 1982, p. C3.

Workman, Andrea. "Twenty American Artists of SFMMA." *West Art,* Aug. 22, 1980.

Zickerman, Lynne. "In Art with Manuel Neri." *Daily Californian Arts Magazine* (Berkeley, CA), Sept. 20, 1972, pp. 12–13, 18.